# ORAL SKILLS FOR S

## CLIENT INTERVIEWING AND NEGOTIATION

Dr Matthew Parry
Amanda Rees

Series editors: Amy and David Sixsmith

REVISE
SQE

First published in 2025 by Fink Publishing Ltd

Impression number 10   9   8   7   6   5   4   3   2

*British Library Cataloguing in Publication Data*
A catalogue record for this book is available from the British Library.
ISBN: 9781917183079

This book is also available in various ebook formats.
Ebook ISBN: 9781917183086

Cover and text design by BMLD (bmld.uk)
Production and typesetting by Westchester Publishing Services UK
Development editing by Llinos Edwards
Video photography by Andy Sixsmith of 6Media
Indexing by Terry Halliday

**Fink Publishing Ltd**
**Email: hello@revise4law.co.uk**
**www.revise4law.co.uk**

**Acknowledgements**
Every effort has been made to obtain necessary permission with reference to copyright material. The publishers apologise if inadvertently any sources remain unacknowledged and will gladly make suitable arrangements with any copyright holders whom it has not been possible to contact.

Extracts from the SRA website in this book are owned by and published under licence from the Solicitors Regulation Authority of The Cube, 199 Wharfside Street, Birmingham, B1 1RN, which asserts its right to be identified as the author of this work in accordance with the Copyright, Designs and Patents Act 1988 Sections 77 and 78: www.sra.org.uk/solicitors/standards-regulations /financial-services-conduct-business-rules/.

Please refer to the SRA website to ensure you are relying upon the correct version and most up-to-date version of the Standards.

**Notes from the publisher**
1. While Fink Publishing has made every attempt to ensure that advice on the qualification and its assessment is accurate, the official specification and associated assessment guidance materials are the only authoritative source of information and should always be referred to for definitive guidance. See the SRA website at https://sqe.sra.org.uk. Note that the SRA may amend their assessment guidance (including the contents of the assessment specifications) at any point.

2. Fink Publishing has robust editorial processes to ensure the accuracy of the content in this publication, and every effort is made to ensure this publication is free of errors. We are, however, only human, and occasionally errors do occur. Fink Publishing is not liable for any misunderstandings that arise as a result of errors in this publication, but it is our priority to ensure that the content is accurate. If you spot an error, please do contact us at **revise4law.co.uk** so we can make sure it is corrected.

# Contents

This book is dedicated to Professor Nancy Schultz (1957–2023), who spent three decades teaching and coaching the interpersonal skills that are essential for any lawyer.

# Contributors

## THE AUTHORS

Dr Matthew Parry is a non-practising solicitor advocate (civil) and a senior lecturer at the Hillary Rodham Clinton School of Law, Swansea University, with research interests in legal education, alternative dispute resolution and land law. He is co-chair of the England and Wales Client Interviewing Competition National Committee and the National Representative of Wales for the International Client Consultation Competition, and coaches law school teams at negotiation competitions on a regular basis.

Matthew's personal journey into skills development would not have been possible without the mentoring of Graham Robson and Professor Julie Price: merci/diolch.

Amanda Rees qualified as a solicitor in 1988, having trained with city firm Radcliffes and Co. She went on to specialise in probate and litigation at Midlands-based firm Perkins and Tustin. She has combined practice and teaching, undertaking personal injury with Swansea-based firm Beor Wilson and Lloyd, and teaching on the undergraduate programme at Swansea University. Amanda is also an SRA external examiner. She has an extensive background in civil litigation and probate, having worked in both city and regional firms. She led the civil litigation and probate modules on the LPC course and also the personal injury and clinical negligence elective. Amanda coordinated the careers and work placement programmes for the LPC and was also the pastoral and disability tutor for the course until 2023.

## SERIES EDITORS

Dr Amy Sixsmith is associate professor in law at the University of Sunderland and a senior fellow of Advance HE.

Dr David Sixsmith is assistant professor in law at Northumbria Law School and a senior fellow of Advance HE.

# Introduction to client interviewing and negotiation

Welcome to *Revise SQE: Legal Skills for SQE2*! This series of revision guides is designed to guide you through the second element of your Solicitors Qualifying Examination, in which you will be tested on your ability to put the legal knowledge you acquired for the SQE1 assessment into different practical contexts.

*Oral Skills for SQE2: Client Interviewing and Negotiation* explores the skills required for the client interview component of the SQE2 oral assessments, focusing first on client interviewing and then on negotiation. The introduction explains what client interviewing is, what it involves and why it is important to the practice of law. The chapter provides detailed guidance on how the skill of client interviewing is assessed in the SQE2 assessments. The SQE2 assessment criteria for client interviewing are explained, alongside the Solicitors Regulatory Authority's (SRA) performance indicators for each criterion, which candidates will need to demonstrate to prove their competency. Two example scenarios are also set out. These will be used throughout the book to provide context to the discussion and guidance.

The central focus of this text is the oral skill of client interviewing. It is also important to note, however, that the SQE2 client interview assessment includes a written element that follows the interview, and you will need to prove your competency in this component to pass the overall assessment. There is a specific discussion of this part of the interviewing assessment in Chapter 4, and we also recommend *Introduction to Written Legal Skills for SQE2* for guidance and advice on developing your writing.

## ■ HOW DOES CLIENT INTERVIEWING FIT INTO THE SQE2 ASSESSMENTS?

### SQE2 WRITTEN AND ORAL SKILLS ASSESSMENTS

SQE2 is split into two parts: oral and written. The table below shows the contexts in which these skills are assessed.

| Part | Skills | Contexts |
|---|---|---|
| Oral | Client interview and attendance note/legal analysis | Property practice<br>Wills and intestacy, probate administration and practice |
| | Advocacy | Dispute resolution<br>Criminal litigation |
| Written | Case and matter analysis<br>Legal research<br>Legal writing<br>Legal drafting | Criminal litigation<br>Dispute resolution<br>Property practice<br>Wills and intestacy, probate administration and practice<br>Business organisations, rules and procedures |

## Oral skills

You will sit four oral skills examinations, which will take place over two half-days.

On day one you will be assessed in:

- advocacy in the context of dispute resolution
- interviewing in the context of property practice.

On day two you will be assessed in:

- advocacy in the context of criminal litigation
- interviewing in the context of wills and intestacy, probate administration and practice.

For the sake of convenience, throughout this book any discussion about property practice will be referred to as 'property' and any discussion about wills and intestacy, probate administration and practice will be referred to as 'wills and probate'.

## Written skills

For the written skills assessment, you will sit 12 examinations that will take place over three half-days. Every day you will be required to take an assessment in each written skill – legal research, case and matter analysis, legal writing and legal drafting.

## ON THE DAY

The process of the assessment is set out on the SRA website. Remember to check the website regularly to ensure that you are up to date with any amendments that have been made.

## Materials

On arrival at the assessment centre, the SRA guidance states that all personal possessions must be left in the secure storage area. Candidates will then be provided with everything they require for the assessment, such as:

- a highlighter pen
- a calculator
- a black ball point pen and
- writing paper.

You will not be permitted to use any other materials. In the SRA's sample videos available on its website, there is a clock in the room so that candidates can keep track of time during the assessment. Watches and phones must be left with the candidates' personal belongings.

Note that you are not permitted to take refreshments into the assessment with you. The SRA's guidance states that water will be provided for candidates and that additional 'light refreshments', such as hot drinks, water, biscuits and fruit, will be available during registration and the scheduled break.

### Reasonable adjustments
If you think that you may require reasonable adjustments for the SQE2 assessments, you must submit a formal request to the SRA. The process for making such a request, together with guidance concerning reasonable adjustments, is set out on the SRA's website at this link: **https://sqe.sra.org.uk/registering-and-booking/reasonable-adjustments**

**The assessment components**

In each SQE2 client interview assessment, your time will be broken down into three components.

---

### 1. PREPARATION: 10 minutes

The SRA guidance states that you will receive a memorandum to read before the interview begins. This is normally an email from a partner in a fictional law firm that (1) provides some context and information on the client and their concern and (2) might contain additional relevant documents. The type of document provided will vary depending on the subject matter being assessed, such as a last will and testament for the wills and probate assessment, and a plan or a Land Registry document for the property assessment.

It is important that you use this time wisely, to familiarise yourself with the information and any supplementary documents that have been provided. Chapter 1 covers this aspect of the assessment.

↓

### 2. THE INTERVIEW: 25 minutes

The interview with the new client then begins, based on the information in the memorandum. The client will be played by the assessor. We recommend approaching the interview as a two-step process: first to gather information and second to formulate your advice. As this is an initial client interview, it is conducted on the basis that preliminary advice should be given to the client, but that detailed advice would follow in the future. Chapters 2 and 3 cover this aspect of the assessment.

↓

### 3. THE ATTENDANCE NOTE/LEGAL ANALYSIS: 25 minutes

When the interview has ended you must write, by hand, an attendance note of the interview. This should summarise your findings from the interview. You need to include all relevant information gleaned from the client and an analysis of the legal matters that arise. The note should flag up any ethical issues and record the preliminary advice that you gave to the client. Finally, you must suggest the next steps for the case, present different options for the client (which could include negotiation) and include advice on specific questions or matters as requested by the partner.

This part of the assessment replicates the real-life expectation for solicitors to make a record of interviews that have taken place so that the case file contains a full record of all dealings with the client. Chapter 4 covers this part of the assessment.

---

## ■ WHY IS INTERVIEWING AN IMPORTANT SKILL FOR A SOLICITOR?

During the course of most cases, a solicitor will need to conduct at least one interview with the relevant parties. Most interviews will be with the client, whether as an initial meeting, to update the client on the case, to advise them on a developing situation or to gain a note of evidence to formulate a witness statement. The SQE2 assessment specifically focuses on the first of these interview examples: the initial meeting with the client. This meeting is significant for many reasons.

1.  All cases will involve an initial interview with a client who is seeking legal advice on a matter that is important to them. In order to understand the nature of the client's issue and to provide some preliminary advice to them, a solicitor must gain information about both the client and the issue upon which they are seeking advice. For the SQE2 assessment, although you will be given some information about the client's issue in the memorandum (see page vii), you will have to deploy effective interviewing skills to gather the detailed information that you need in order to provide initial legal advice to the client.

### Assessment technique

The interview is the only opportunity that you have to ask questions to ensure that your preliminary advice in the attendance note is as accurate as possible. Once the client has left, your chance to gain information has also disappeared!

2.  The SRA sets national standards for solicitors, monitors performance, and implements and enforces rules of professional conduct so that the public can have confidence in the profession. Although solicitors will adopt slightly different approaches to interviewing clients, there are some points that must be covered in order to comply with professional obligations, as set out in the SRA Code of Conduct for Solicitors. You can access the Code on the SRA's website but here are examples of some points that must be included in an initial interview:

    -   the duty of confidentiality that a solicitor owes to their client
    -   contact information for the client
    -   the solicitor's role in the firm
    -   the relevant complaints procedure.

    The assessment criteria for the client interview make no reference to the opening of the interview during which these client care points would normally be covered; neither are they included in the sample interviews provided by the SRA on its website. In these sample interviews, the candidate asks two questions to confirm the client's preferred method of contact and then moves straight into asking questions about the case. However, the distinction between professional conduct issues and client care issues is not always clear-cut. At the beginning of a client interview, you would normally spend a few minutes of introductions to the client, establishing your professional relationship with them and so on. The SRA's sample interviews meet the threshold for a pass, suggesting that in the assessment candidates do not need to spend much time on introductions. In this book, we do suggest that concisely covering some introductory matters may help you to demonstrate that you meet the assessment criteria for client interviewing (explored in more detail on page x) and the SRA's objective for you to 'win the client's trust and confidence'. As guidance, the SRA website includes this 'note to candidates':

    > You should consider professional conduct issues, as appropriate. You do not need to deal with client care, money laundering, or client identity issues, as the partner has already dealt with these.

3.  Finally, the interview that you will be conducting is not with an automaton – it is with a human being. It is important that you remember this, even in the artificial assessment situation where you will be dealing with an assessor actor rather than someone who has experienced these particular issues. In a real-life interview, a solicitor needs to show empathy and build a rapport with their client: for the SQE2 assessment, you will be specifically assessed on your ability to put the client at ease, build trust and establish professional rapport under assessment criterion (**AC**) **3** (see page xi for commentary on the assessment criteria).

This is particularly important for the client seeking advice in respect of wills and estates, as this topic inevitably addresses the emotive topic of death and you will need to demonstrate sensitivity and empathy. Whatever the topic, the client may be very worried or upset about their issue: for example, in a property dispute, there could be significant and long-term consequences, and your client might be concerned about them. It is therefore important to establish and maintain a professional rapport right from the start. The better rapport you have with the client, the more likely it is that they will be prepared to share highly personal and sensitive information during the interview that you will need to understand and assess their case.

## Interview technique

In order to build a rapport with the client, remember to listen closely to information that they provide in answer to your questions. Any response you give should be tailored to that information. Avoid sticking to a memorised script or a predetermined list of questions. A key interviewing skill is the ability to listen and respond – to think on your feet and be flexible. See Chapter 2 for guidance and support on asking the right sort of questions to extract the information you need from the client.

## ■ CLIENT INTERVIEWING ASSESSMENT CRITERIA AND COMMENTARY

There are separate assessment criteria for the client interview component and the attendance note/legal analysis component.

- The goal of the *client interview* component of the assessment is purely skills-orientated: marks are awarded only on the skill of interviewing and not on the accuracy of the legal advice. This is underpinned by the objective of this component, which is to be 'able to conduct an interview with a client' and by the assessment criteria below, taken from the SRA website. You need to be very familiar with all aspects of these assessment criteria, so that you can bear them in mind on the day and make sure that you are achieving each point.
- The goal of the *attendance note* component of the assessment is to record all relevant information obtained during the interview. You should also provide an analysis of any legal issues that arise in the matter and record your initial advice for the client. In particular, you should focus on the next steps that the client could take and address any specific questions raised by the client, either in the interview or in the attendance note.

We will explore the assessment criteria for the attendance note/legal analysis in Chapter 4. Below is a commentary on the assessment criteria for client interviewing. This part of the SQE2 assessment is covered in detail in Chapters 1, 2 and 3.

## SQE2 client interviewing assessment criteria

Try to remember these points as you conduct the client interview:

### Skills

1. Listen to the client and use questioning effectively to enable the client to tell the solicitor what is important to them.
2. Communicate and explain in a way that is suitable for the client to understand.
3. Conduct themselves in a professional manner and treat the client with courtesy, respect and politeness including respecting diversity where relevant.

4. Demonstrate client-focus in their approach to the client and the issues (ie demonstrate an understanding of the problem from the client's point of view and what the client wants to achieve, not just from a legal perspective).

5. Establish and maintain an effective relationship with the client so as to build trust and confidence.

Let's look more closely at each of these criteria and explore the SRA's standard of competency as described in their performance indicators for SQE2 client interviewing. (See the Appendix for a full record of the SRA's performance indicators in respect of these criteria.)

## SKILLS ASSESSMENT CRITERIA

### 1. Listen to the client and use questioning effectively to enable the client to tell the solicitor what is important to them

In an initial client interview, the client knows the facts of the case and has opinions on the matter but does not necessarily have the expertise to know how best to proceed. As a Day One Solicitor, you have the expertise to identify and resolve legal problems but require the relevant information to be able to do these things. In order to understand the client's situation and offer initial advice, you need to extract relevant information from the client. You will achieve this by establishing a good rapport, asking appropriate questions and utilising effective listening skills to process the information the client provides. Detailed guidance on developing your listening skills and using questions effectively is provided in Chapter 2.

You will demonstrate **competence** if you:

- demonstrate active listening skills and engage with the client
- ask appropriate questions
- use a combination of closed and open questions.

You will **not** demonstrate **competence** if you:

- appear uninterested in the client and fail to engage with them
- do not address the client's concern because you are not listening closely enough, and instead focus on your own agenda
- do not ask appropriate or relevant questions
- use only closed questions, so that the client cannot explain what is important to them.

### 2. Communicate and explain in a way that is suitable for the client to understand

Understanding the situation and knowing the potential options for the client are not enough: in order to meet the threshold for competency, you must communicate and explain information to the client clearly and concisely, in a way that they can understand. You should avoid using overly technical or legalistic language where possible and ensure that any legal terms you have to use are explained clearly to the client. Remember that your client is a layperson who is unlikely to understand complex legal language. In the SQE2 assessment, you should ignore the fact that the person playing the role of client is an assessor who probably has a background in law, and treat them as an ordinary member of the public. Further guidance on communicating with your client is given in Chapter 3.

You will demonstrate **competence** if you:

- use language that is easy to understand
- explain legal terms clearly and succinctly where it is necessary to use technical vocabulary.

You will **not** demonstrate **competence** if you:

- offer explanations which are complicated, long-winded and difficult to understand
- use technical language when necessary but do not explain what these legal terms mean.

## 3. Conduct themselves in a professional manner and treat the client with courtesy, respect and politeness including respecting diversity where relevant

Respecting the client is a central thread that runs through the SRA's Statement of Solicitor Competence (see page xiii) and it is easy to demonstrate in an interview setting. Following simple practices such as asking how the client would like to be addressed, explaining how the interview will run and clarifying that they have understood your advice will demonstrate your professionalism and courtesy towards the client.

Treating the client with respect during the interview is vital for building a rapport with them, which in turn will encourage them to trust you with information about their case and thereby allow you to provide them with preliminary advice.

You will demonstrate **competence** if you:

- are sensitive when delivering difficult news
- treat the client with respect and courtesy
- can build a rapport with the client and behave politely
- can focus on the client's problem but keep a professional distance
- are calm, efficient and well organised.

You will **not** demonstrate **competence** if you:

- are consistently insensitive towards the client
- behave casually towards the client, being flippant or too familiar
- cannot behave politely, and are rude, patronising or disrespectful
- are too hesitant, rushed or flustered, not in control of the situation.

## 4. Demonstrate client-focus in their approach to the client and the issues

Criterion 4 ensures that the client is at the centre of the interview. It requires you to demonstrate an understanding of the problem from the client's point of view and what the client wants to achieve, not just their legal position. It is fundamentally important that your advice is tailored specifically to the client that you are interviewing, rather than to another scenario that might be similar in some ways but not all.

In addition to gathering facts and information, you also need to gain a clear understanding of the client's aims and objectives. This is crucial because it may impact the advice you offer. For example, if a client comes to you for advice regarding a dispute with their neighbour but states that they wish to make amends rather than escalate matters, advice that focuses on litigation against that neighbour is unlikely to demonstrate a focus on the client's concerns, no matter how strong the legal case. Litigation is likely to have an adverse impact on the relationship between the client and their neighbour, so if you explore other mediatory avenues in the first instance this would demonstrate an understanding of the issue from the client's perspective.

Do not presume to know what the client wants or needs. You must always take the time to understand the client's viewpoint and what they want to achieve. Having this understanding allows you to provide the client with information that enables them to make an informal decision about how to proceed. For example, if the client is worried about resolving an issue very quickly then you might need to explain the timeframes involved in litigation.

This criterion also specifically refers to the importance of non-legal options. The central role of a solicitor is that of a problem-solver, and it is important that the client is provided not only with an outline of potential legal remedies but also with alternative, practical options that might be more effective in resolving the issue.

You will demonstrate **competence** if you:

- show that you can understand the client's problem from their perspective
- can empathise with the client over their concern.

You will **not** demonstrate **competence** if you:

- cannot approach the client's issue from their perspective
- cannot empathise with the client
- do not take the client's concerns into consideration when offering advice.

### 5. Establish and maintain an effective relationship with the client so as to build trust and confidence

Again, the relationship between the candidate and the client is central here and, to a degree, underpins all the other criteria. Throughout the interview, right from the very start to the end, you must demonstrate that you have established and maintained an effective relationship with the client. The client should feel that they have been treated well, understand the possible options and limitations for their case, and can trust you to handle the specific situation.

You will demonstrate **competence** if you:

- can manage the client's expectations, in terms of likely outcomes and timeframe
- instil confidence in the client that you will be able to resolve their issue.

You will **not** demonstrate **competence** if you:

- over-promise and fail to manage the client's expectations
- are unable to give the client confidence that you can progress this matter.

## ■ FUNCTIONING LEGAL KNOWLEDGE

Unlike the assessment criteria for the written skills components of SQE2, the client interviewing assessment criteria do not include 'application of law'. The interviewing component is a skills-based assessment but that is not to say that the law should be disregarded. Whilst inaccurate knowledge or a poor grasp of the law will not by itself lead to lower marks according to the assessment criteria, it will make it more difficult for you to formulate questions and respond to information the client gives.

| Assessment technique |
| --- |
| Do not be complacent! A good knowledge and grasp of the subject area will make it much easier to formulate questions or lines of questioning and pre-empt possible issues or questions the client might ask. |

Furthermore, the SQE2 assessment is underpinned by the Statement of Solicitor Competence, which is a list of requirements that a solicitor must fulfil to perform their role effectively. Lack of legal knowledge could hinder a solicitor's ability to demonstrate their competency. For example:

- Competency B3 requires the solicitor to give the client appropriate options. Your knowledge of the law should lead you to give your client sound advice, but if you erroneously believe that they have a very strong legal position you might encourage them to litigate, when in fact this should not be advised if their legal position is weak. Chapter 1 emphasises the importance of tailoring different options to the client's specific needs and circumstances.
- Competency B6 requires the solicitor to understand how and when it might be appropriate to negotiate solutions to clients' issues. As will be seen in Chapter 5, an important aspect of this skill is understanding when negotiation may or may not be a feasible option for the client. If your understanding of negotiation is not accurate, your advice will be weak and incorrect.
- Without sound legal knowledge it will also be harder to satisfy the category C competencies. These competencies require clear and confident communication with other people, in this case the client. If you understand the legal position and are confident in the accuracy of your legal advice, you will be able to explain the position more clearly to the client and give them confidence in your capability.

To illustrate these points: if the issue in a wills and probate interview assessment concerns the validity of the will and you advise that the will has been correctly executed when in fact it has not, you will ignore a range of possibilities including negotiation, and leave the client with an inaccurate impression of the situation. In practice, this could damage the trust your client has in your ability to manage their case. In the context of the SQE2 assessment, it may adversely impact your performance because you fail to outline an appropriate range of solutions to the client's problem; this would not demonstrate a client-focused approach as required by **AC 4**.

---

### SQE1 functioning legal knowledge link

If you need to revise the law relating to property or wills/probate, see our SQE1 revision guides for these areas: *Revise SQE: Wills and the Administration of Estates* and *Revise SQE: Property Practice*.

---

## ■ HOW IS SQE2 MARKED?

Each of the SQE2 skills has its own set of assessment criteria. The client interview assessment is marked against the criteria explored on pages x–xiii using the following scale:

A. Superior performance: well above the competency requirements of the assessment.
B. Clearly satisfactory: clearly meets the competency requirements of the assessment.
C. Marginal pass: on balance, just meets the competency requirements of the assessment.
D. Marginal fail: on balance, just fails to meet the competency requirements of the assessment.
E. Clearly unsatisfactory: clearly does not meet the competency requirements of the assessment.
F. Poor performance: well below the competency requirements of the assessment.

Your mark will be calculated by converting the grade into a numerical mark, with A representing 5 marks and F representing 0 marks.

## The scaled scoring system

In January 2025 the SRA introduced a scaled scoring system for all SQE2 assessments. This approach is designed to ensure that candidate scores are comparable across different assessment sittings, thereby providing a fair and consistent measure of candidate performance. The same system has already been implemented for all SQE1 assessments.

The scaled scoring system works in the following way:

- Initially, candidates will receive a 'raw score' based on their performance across the 16 assessment stations in SQE2.
- A pass mark is then set for each assessment window. The pass mark is determined using statistical methods that account for any differences in question difficulty. This ensures fairness across different exam versions.
- Candidate raw scores are then converted to a common scale ranging from 0 to 500, with the pass mark consistently set at 300. This standardisation allows for direct comparisons between candidates' performances, regardless of the specific assessments they completed.

When you access your results, you will be able to see:

- a detailed breakdown of your results by assessment station (results will be expressed as marks from 0 to 5 for each assessment criterion across each of the 16 assessment stations)
- your overall mark expressed as a percentage
- your scaled score out of 500 – remember that the pass mark will always be set at 300.

For more information about the scaled scoring system, visit the SRA's website.

It is very important that you are aware of the standard you are required to meet. The competence standard is that of a Day One Solicitor, which is mapped against Level 3 of the Threshold Standard for the Statement of Solicitor Competence. This is available on the SRA website and we would encourage you to review this prior to sitting your SQE2 assessment.

## The assessors

In terms of who will be assessing you against this standard, and the relevant skills criteria, the interview will be marked by the person you are interviewing, whilst the remaining assessments (attendance note, advocacy and all written skills) will be marked by a solicitor. All assessors will have received training on how to assess a candidate's performance against the relevant criteria. It is therefore essential that you tackle your assessments in the same way that you would if you were a fully qualified solicitor on the first day of practice – with professionalism, confidence and calmness. This will come across to your assessor during your SQE2 assessment: remember that they are assessing whether you are adequately equipped to begin working in legal practice.

## ■ CLIENT INTERVIEWING SKILLS IN CONTEXT

## WORKED EXAMPLES

Throughout this book, reference will be made to two examples in order to provide context for the guidance provided – **Example 1** relating to the wills and probate interview, and **Example 2** to the property interview. The details for both cases are given below:

| Example 1: wills and probate |
|---|
| James Smith has come to see you for advice regarding his father Simon's estate. Simon died earlier this month. He had not made a will at the time of his death and therefore died intestate. At the time of his death, Simon was divorced and had two living children, James and Lucy. He was living with his partner, Angela. |

| Example 2: property |
|---|
| Yusuf Ahmed has come to see you regarding a potential dispute with his neighbour, Klara Marks. He believes that he has a right to own part of his neighbour's land and wants to know what he can do about it before he sells the property. Both his land and his neighbour's land are registered. |

## PRACTICE INTERVIEW ASSESSMENTS

Chapters 7 and 8 contain practice client interview assessments in wills/probate and property law. In both chapters, you are provided with a memorandum (similar to the memo you would receive in the SQE2 client interview assessments) and a client brief so that another person can play the role of client. You have the opportunity to engage in two practice interviews, and then you can watch the accompanying videos to see examples of how the interviews might proceed. We reflect on the success of those interviews and how they achieve and demonstrate different elements of the assessment criteria. The videos can be viewed at **https://revise4law.co.uk/sqe2-interviewing-video/**, and a full transcript is given in each chapter.

## ◼ SUMMARY AND REFLECTION

This introduction has provided some general guidance about the oral component of the SQE2 client interview assessment. The remaining chapters will explore the following aspects of this assessment:

- Chapter 1: preparing for the interview in the ten-minute preparation time.
- Chapter 2: the opening and information-gathering stages of the interview, where you develop a professional rapport and seek information from the client by asking a series of questions.
- Chapter 3: the part of the interview where you advise the client of the law and their options, and then draw the interview to a close.
- Chapter 4: the written attendance note/legal analysis that forms part of the assessment.
- Chapter 5: how to approach negotiation.
- Chapter 6: examples of interview skills in practice, with commentary.
- Chapters 7 and 8: practice client interview assessments for you to attempt.

It is important to remember that it is not possible to provide you with guidance on how to conduct the perfect interview, because every solicitor will have a different view of what this might contain. The book provides guidance to help you prepare for and conduct an interview that satisfies the SQE2 assessment criteria. It does so by exploring the skills required and providing you with a range of tools to improve the quality of your interviews and attendance notes/legal analyses.

# Preparing to conduct the initial client interview

In the introduction we looked at the specific skills required for client interviewing and explained their importance in practice. We also outlined how client interviewing is assessed in the SQE2 assessment. The next three chapters focus on how to conduct the interview in a manner that is likely to satisfy the assessment criteria for SQE2:

- This chapter provides guidance, first, on how to prepare yourself and plan for the client interview assessment, and second on how best to utilise the ten-minute preparation time before meeting the client in the assessment.
- Chapter 2 focuses on the early stages of the interview, where you need to develop a professional relationship with the client and gather information from them.
- Chapter 3 examines the later stages of the interview, where you will give legal and non-legal (practical) advice to the client and then conclude the interview.

These parts of the interview will be placed into context, with specific reference to the type of interview that you may have to conduct in the assessment. Although the guidance is relevant for all topics that may arise during client interviews in practice, there is specific focus on wills/probate and property, as you will need to conduct an interview on each of these topics for the SQE2 assessment.

The advice given in these three chapters is clearly linked to the SQE2 assessment criteria for client interviewing as outlined in the introduction. When developing your skills, always bear in mind the SRA's straightforward objective for this assessment:

> In the interview candidates should aim to win the client's trust and confidence. They should try to obtain all the relevant information and as full an understanding as possible of the client's concerns.

## ■ GENERAL PREPARATION FOR THE CLIENT INTERVIEW ASSESSMENT

Preparing for a client interview can be daunting for a Day One Solicitor in practice. The added pressure of the SQE2 interviews being assessed adds to the tension, and this is magnified by the fact that the 'client' that you are interviewing is also the assessor who is determining whether or not you will pass the SQE2 assessment.

This pressure can affect people in different ways and, like any examination, nerves can adversely impact performance on the day. This section provides guidance and tips to help you manage your nerves so that you can feel, or at least appear to be, relaxed, confident and capable during the interview.

**Assessment technique**

Although this is a different kind of assessment to a written examination, of which you will have much more experience, you might be able to draw on similar techniques as you prepare for the assessment. For example: get a good night's sleep before the assessment; make sure you arrive early at the assessment centre to avoid rushing at the last minute; breathe slowly to calm your nerves before the assessment begins. You will have your own approach to assessments and know what works best for you!

## PRACTISE BEING AN INTERVIEWER

The simple fact is that there is no better way to prepare for this assessment than to practise it as much as you can. There are many ways that you can do this.

- If you are using a formal training provider to prepare for SQE2, they might offer opportunities to practise this skill and provide formative feedback on your performance in the interview.
- You may know other candidates on the same course who would be prepared to work with you by playing the role of a client whilst you play the solicitor, with you swapping roles with them to give them the same opportunity.
- Ask a friend or family member to help you by playing the role of the client. The SRA's website provides an example of the type of information that the client will be given in advance of the interview. It is vital to note that you, the interviewer, will not have access to this information before, during or after the SQE2 assessment. These materials may, however, be a useful resource when practising for your assessment. Whoever will play the client in your practice interview(s) can use them to get acquainted with the facts in order to play the role effectively. Chapters 7 and 8 contain practice client interview assessments for you to attempt, including client briefs for the person playing the role of client.
- You could also ask family members, friends or peers to make up their own legal problems for you to discuss and address in an interview, such as an issue/query concerning a will, or a property-based neighbour dispute. This can be a helpful way of testing whether you gain a good understanding of the client's legal issue, concerns and objectives.

The main purpose of practising is for you to understand what it feels like to be in the position of interviewing someone in this setting. One of the hardest parts of the client interview is to take the theory, or what you know you should say, and actually put it into words when looking at the other person across the table. By practising in this way, you can ensure that the first time you say 'Hello, I am a solicitor' is not in the assessment itself. Practising in mock interviews will help to build your confidence and this will translate into a confident client interview. The practice interview assessment materials in Chapters 7 and 8 should help you to practise your skills in simulated client interviews.

**Interview technique**

When you conduct a practice interview, always ask for feedback. It would be ideal if the interviewee could judge how you performed against the SQE2 assessment criteria on page x and decide whether you achieved the standard threshold. However, if they cannot do this, they should still be able to tell you whether you managed to get all the information from them, whether they understood your explanation of their options, and whether they felt at ease and confident in your ability to manage their case. This will help you to identify areas of strength and improvement. Their responses to the following questions will indicate how well you communicated on a personal level:

- Were your questions clear?
- Were your explanations understandable?
- Were you able to gather all of the relevant information?
- Did you outline the options clearly, and provide advantages and disadvantages of each?
- What did they think of your body language? Did you make them feel at ease, or did you annoy them, eg by rolling your eyes or not smiling?
- Did you treat them with respect and sincerity, and did you start to build up a rapport with them?

Receiving this kind of feedback will help you to become a better interviewer, and to approach the SQE2 assessment with a style that works for you and enhances your confidence.

## PRACTISE BEING A CLIENT

This second piece of advice is most likely to be relevant if you have a friend or peer who is also preparing for the SQE2 assessment and wants to practise their own interviewing skills. Although it will be enormously helpful for you to interview them as the interviewee, do not underestimate the potential benefits of playing the role of the client for them to interview, particularly if you cover the same case information as interviewer and interviewee.

Being a client in a mock interview allows you to see the impact that questions and comments have upon you, and might lead you to reflect on your approach. For example, as an interviewer, you may think that the question 'How much do you earn?' is relevant and reasonable, so that you can determine the potential for a claim in certain situations. However, when you are playing the role of the client and have that question directed at you, you will probably see that in certain situations it could make you feel uncomfortable and awkward, particularly if you have come to see the solicitor about a sensitive topic.

### Assessment technique

Remember the performance indicators for **AC 3**: your competency in SQE2 will depend on being sensitive and treating the client with respect. See page xii for commentary on this assessment criterion, and the Appendix for full details of the performance indicators.

You are more likely to recognise and understand the need for sensitivity by being on the receiving end of the questions, and you will learn how certain interviewing strategies and techniques can have an impact on the client's experience.

### Interview technique

When you are deciding what to say in an interview, think about how the client might construe it. This might be different from how you mean it to be heard. By practising being a client, you will understand how what is *heard* can sometimes be different from what is *said*, because your tone of voice can affect the way in which the client interprets your words.

## REMEMBER THAT THE ASSESSMENT REPLICATES A CLIENT INTERVIEW

A common misconception is that live assessments like this one are designed to trip you up on your lack of knowledge. That is not the case, and this is reflected in the SRA's assessment objective for client interviewing:

Candidates can demonstrate they are able to conduct an interview with a client.

In practice, most clients are genuinely seeking help, and the client interview assessment seeks to replicate this. The client/assessor does not wish you to fail and, although there may be issues that are not straightforward and require careful consideration, the assessments will only cover topics that are set out on the SRA website for the functioning legal knowledge (FLK) of the SQE1 assessment for property and wills/probate. The key point to note is that the interviewing assessment is designed to test your ability to conduct an interview.

If you do feel nervous about the assessment, do not be afraid to tell yourself out loud that you *can* do this! Be reassured that the purpose of this assessment is to test your existing skills, not to trick you by containing something you did not expect.

## REVISE THE RELEVANT LAW

The oral assessments pose two important challenges:

1. As mentioned in the introduction, you cannot take any personal possessions into the interview. You are permitted to take the notes that you made upon receiving the email from your partner during the ten minutes of preparation time, but not other pre-prepared notes to remind yourself of the assessment criteria, possible structure, timings, approaches to take and so on.
2. Although you will know whether the client is coming to see you about a property or a wills and probate issue, you will not have any additional information about the client or the nature of their problem until you receive the email ten minutes before the interview begins. There is therefore a limit to how much you can prepare for the specific topic of each interview.

---

**SQE1 functioning legal knowledge link**

As we recommended in the introduction, you need to ensure that your knowledge of the relevant subjects (property and wills and probate) is up to date, to enable you to feel confident in providing legal advice in your SQE2 assessments. Keep checking the SRA website for updates and see our SQE1 revision guides for these areas: *Revise SQE: Wills and the Administration of Estates* and *Revise SQE: Property Practice*.

---

Although we recommend that you review the relevant FLK for these two topics, there is no expectation that you will know and be able to recall the finer details of the relevant law. Again, remember two central points from the SQE2 assessment specification as displayed on the SRA's website:

- Candidates will be marked on skills only.
- Candidates 'will need sufficient knowledge to make them competent to practise on the basis that they can look up detail later'.

Source: **https://sqe.sra.org.uk/exam-arrangements/assessment-information/sqe2-assessment-specification**

Your priority therefore should be to ensure that you have a clear understanding of the *general principles* within the relevant subject areas rather than focusing on the precise detail. For an example relating to inheritance tax for wills and estates, it is important to know that lifetime gifts constitute a potentially exempt transfer except in certain specific situations, and that the liability reduces as the time between the gift and the date of death increases until it becomes exempt at seven years. However, you do not need to be as concerned about memorising the precise years that taper relief applies, or the amount of the tax relief that applies at those points. You could make a point in your attendance note that these details should be looked up later.

A broad knowledge of the subject area and general principles will allow you to develop a rough plan for what type of questions you might ask if certain types of problem arise, and this will help to overcome the challenges outlined above. For example:

- If the will has been signed by someone who is also a beneficiary, you will need to ask questions about validity and explain this issue to the client.
- If the property assessment is about a neighbour dispute, you will need to ask questions about boundaries and the client's relationship with their neighbour.

---

**Assessment technique**

Remember, the more that you practise client interviewing, the more confident you will feel discussing property and wills/probate issues. If you only focus your time and effort on memorising the law and do not practise your interviewing skills, you are less likely to feel comfortable and confident when you conduct the SQE2 assessments.

---

Let's look more closely at the two subject areas examinable on the SQE2 interviewing assessments, as each raises distinct issues that require you to adopt different interviewing styles/techniques.

## Wills and probate

The SRA's sample question on wills and probate on its website indicates the type of case that will be presented. For this assessment, it is highly likely that the client will have recently lost a friend or family member and requires advice, either because there is no will or there is a potential problem with a will. You can isolate many of the key areas of law likely to be relevant here and revise your legal knowledge: see Chapter 3, where the advice section of the interview is discussed. In preparing for this assessment, you will need to ensure that you can confidently advise clients in situations where (1) there is a valid will, (2) there is no legitimate will, and (3) there is no will at all; this is therefore an obvious area of the law to revise.

We also recommend thinking ahead about the type of information that you would need to gather from your client in this type of situation. For example, one of the crucial tasks in this assessment might be to understand the contents of the estate. These can normally be broken down into categories, such as:

- assets – eg cash, bank accounts, stocks and shares, personal possessions, insurance policies and pensions
- liabilities – eg funeral expenses and other debts.

By identifying potential aspects of an estate to enquire about before the assessment, you put yourself in a strong position to gain all the information you need from your client during the interview. This will enable you to get a good understanding of the nature and extent of the estate in question.

The range of issues that could appear in the wills/probate assessments is quite limited, because of the nature of the law in this area. There is a logical progression that can be followed to ensure that you cover all of the relevant points. The best starting point is to understand how a will can be valid or invalid, and then you can consider the technicalities (ie number of executors and whether they are available and willing to act in that capacity). If the scenario involves property, you will need to understand how that property was held or is currently held, in order to advise on the consequences for the property and, by extension, inheritance tax, along with the situations where individual gifts may be within the estate or outside the estate, and what happens if they are no longer in existence.

It is also important that you consider the rules that govern situations when the deceased has died intestate and potential claims are made under the Inheritance (Provision for Family and Dependants) Act 1975. Although the details of the client's issue and their reason for seeking advice will vary in different assessments, this particular topic is largely governed by clear rules. You should be able to ask direct, closed questions, confident that your client will be able to give you sufficient information in their response (at least to the extent of the required FLK for this assessment). Ensuring that you are familiar with these rules, which can be identified from the advice section in Chapter 3, will help you to prepare for the interview itself.

| Example 1: wills and probate |
|---|
| Refer back to the details on page xv: you are told that James Smith died without a will. If you were presented with this scenario in your assessment, you would immediately need to draw on your knowledge of the rules of intestacy, rather than the detailed rules for determining the validity of a will. This would enable you to plan lines of questioning for the interview. |

## Property

The SQE2 client interview on property is, arguably, more difficult to prepare for because the subject matter is much broader. For example, advising on a boundary dispute is very different from advising on a title issue: the former covers the extent of ownership of land and potentially adverse possession, whilst the latter requires a very precise understanding of the legal title itself.

Despite this greater range of potential topics for assessment, it is useful to prepare for some key property law principles so that you can approach the assessment with confidence. For example:

- Consider how you would explain some of the complicated concepts of land law to a client, such as easements and covenants.
- Build your confidence in talking about concepts of ownership and mortgages.
- Make sure you understand and can explain what conveyancing entails and the different stages involved in the process.

| Example 2: property |
|---|
| Refer back to the details on page xv: you are told that Yusuf Ahmed wishes to establish a right to land that is legally owned by his neighbour. Whilst there are a number of possible legal issues, the most likely is adverse possession, and therefore it would be logical to focus your questioning on this issue. |

## IT IS JUST A CONVERSATION!

Although the SQE2 initial client interview is assessed and should be conducted in a professional manner, remember that all client interviews are essentially conversations. Over the course of your life you will have often introduced yourself to strangers, talked about topics that you know well, learned about what is important to them, and possibly given your opinion. At its very core, this interview assessment is the same. Obviously for this interview you need to follow some guidelines on what to say and how to phrase it carefully, but if you are feeling nervous it might help you to think about this interview as just another human interaction: an opportunity for you to draw on your own interpersonal skills and use your expertise to help another person.

## ■ THE CLIENT INTERVIEW ASSESSMENT: THE ALLOCATED PREPARATION TIME

The final stage of your preparation for the interview is the ten-minute period after you receive the memorandum in the SQE2 assessment: an email that sets out a summary of the client that you are about to interview, possibly accompanied by some documents. This is such a short period of time that you might think you can achieve little other than identifying the basic details of the client that you will be speaking to. This is a good start but it is essential to use this time efficiently to extract as much information as you can about this case.

---

### Assessment technique: do not panic!

The most important thing is not to panic. Many candidates might do so when they read the memorandum for the first time – you might be nervous about the assessment and concerned that your revision has not prepared you sufficiently for the client interview. But during this crucial ten-minute window it is important not to waste valuable time worrying about what you have not done and instead to focus on what you can achieve.

When you receive the memorandum, try to remain as calm as possible. Some candidates might prefer to dive straight in and start reading; others might want to take three deep breaths before doing so. Whatever technique you choose to adopt, it is vital that you are able to read, digest and understand the information.

If you find that you are looking at the words but not processing the information, try to reset: stop reading, look away, try to calm your nerves by using a technique you have already practised and know works for you, and then look again at the memorandum. By forcing yourself to restart, you will increase your chances of being able to comprehend the information properly.

---

## IDENTIFY THE CORE ISSUES

When you have read the memorandum once, read it again and annotate the document, focusing on the central points, for example:

- who your client is
- their address, if one is provided
- any relevant personal circumstances – and particularly for a wills and probate question, their relation to the person recently deceased, if there is one
- the issue that they wish to discuss with you

- any information that may be relevant to additional advice that they seek, for example references to the goals of the client, or any particular concerns that are identified. In particular, look out for references to additional documents that the client may bring with them (eg a will, Land Registry document or plan).

This is not an exhaustive list and every candidate will have their own preference for how they note the core issues. However, try to avoid underlining every single sentence of the memorandum as this will defeat one of the objects of the exercise – to have an easy reference point when you are interviewing the client (see Chapters 2 and 3) and/or writing your attendance note (see Chapter 4).

## INSPECT ANY DOCUMENTS

The guidance provided by the SRA makes it clear that additional documents may be attached to the memorandum.

- In the wills and probate question, a will might be included. In **Example 1: wills and probate** on page xv, there is no documentation because the client's father died without a will. However, the practice assessment in Chapter 7 includes a will, which is the sort of document you might be given.
- For the property interview, you could be provided with a short excerpt from a lease, a plan of the property or a copy of the Land Registry title documents. In **Example 2: property** on page xv, although no document is included here, the client might have a copy of title plan with them that would show the boundaries between their property and their neighbour's property.

Examples of the documents that might be attached to the memorandum can be seen in the SRA sample questions on their website: a will for the question on wills and probate and a lease for the property question.

If a document is provided, it is essential that you review it in as much detail as possible within these ten minutes of preparation time. You need to avoid spending too much time reading it during the interview, as this will adversely affect your ability to maintain eye contact and talk to the client, negatively impacting your rapport with them (bear in mind the performance indicators for **AC 3** here, conducting yourself in a professional manner).

Reviewing the document will give you the chance to gather additional information about the case, such as whether the will appears to be valid and what the Land Registry title documentation tells you about the land in question. It will also allow you to focus attention on points that might arise. For example, in the wills and probate interview:

- A will might provide for specific bequests of money and/or items, and will include details of individuals and/or items that you might need to ask questions about.
- You will be able to determine whether the will is valid or not by considering the signatures at the end of the will.
- You will also be able to see if your client is one of the proposed executors or a beneficiary, which will indicate the nature of advice that is being sought, ie as an executor or a potential beneficiary.

In the property interview, supplementary documentation might help you to identify the nature of the client's issue. For example:

- A plan of relevant boundaries might suggest that the advice being sought concerns a boundary dispute or adverse possession claim.

- If the document is a title deed, you should be able to see whether the legal owner matches the name of your client, whether there are any co-owners, and whether there are any easements or covenants on the deed that the client may be seeking advice on.

Reading the email carefully, together with any related documents, will provide you with useful information that can form a strong foundation for your interview. Within that ten-minute period, you might be able to discover who your client is, their status in the case and what they are seeking advice on. You might even be able to identify some of the central issues or potential complications that you will need to explore.

However, try not to panic if the email and/or documents do not enable you to identify the issue in question. You should be able to gather the necessary information in the interview – and remember that you do not need to give accurate legal advice to pass!

## ANTICIPATE THE LIKELY SUBJECT MATTER OF THE INTERVIEW

As you work rapidly to identify the crucial information in your review of the email and associated documents, you should also be able to anticipate the client's issue. This is the first step to achieving **AC 4**: demonstrating client-focus in your approach. Whilst you might not be absolutely certain about what will follow in the interview, you should be able to eliminate a number of possibilities very quickly, even if at first glance the question appears to be broad in nature. You should also then be able to predict the reason for your client to be seeking advice. For example, in a wills and probate assessment:

- If you are given a will that you can see is valid, you are less likely to be concerned with intestacy provisions.
- If the client is named as an executor of the will, you will need to discuss whether they are willing to take on the responsibilities of that role.
- If there are no specific bequests of items in the will, you will not need to make enquiries about whether or not those items continue to exist.
- If there are specific bequests, it will be logical to recall the provisions should those gifts fail for any reason. In particular you should consider the difference between specific legacies and deemed legacies in respect of ademption. (See chapter 3, *Revise SQE Wills and the Administration of Estates* if you need to review your knowledge of this point.)

Likewise, for a property assessment:

- If a title deed is provided, you will probably be focusing on registered land rather than provisions for unregistered land.
- If the email states that the client is seeking advice about a boundary dispute, reading the documentation should allow you to narrow the range of possible issues that you will need to explore.

When you know the nature of the case in either wills/probate or property assessment, you should have a reasonable idea of whether or not your advice might need to include negotiation (see Chapter 5 for guidance on this aspect of the SQE2 assessment). The existence of another party as a potential antagonist will be a good indication that negotiation might be a potential option.

Crucially, if you are concerned about having to hold several possibilities in your mind at once during this preparation stage, be reassured that by methodically reflecting on the information provided you should be able to rule out a few potential topics/issues and be confident that they will not form the subject matter of the interview.

## SKETCH OUT AN INTERVIEW PLAN

Finally – and this might be in the last minute or two of your preparation time – try to use the information given in the memorandum and documents to draw up an interview plan. For example, for a probate interview you might sketch the following points:

1.  Welcome; offer condolences for loss.
2.  Ask for main concerns.
3.  Gather personal information.
4.  Gather financial information (assets and liabilities).
5.  Explain the validity of the will.
6.  Go through the will issue by issue (note particular points).
7.  Clarify status of any issues.
8.  Answer any questions.
9.  Explain next steps.

You might already have a general plan for how you want to conduct the interview but the memorandum information and documents will allow you to plan when to make specific points and prioritise some topics over others. For example, if you know that the client is named as an executor, you will want to establish relatively early in the interview whether or not they are prepared to take on this role, as this will affect the practical advice you give later in the assessment. In practice this would also indicate whether they will be a continuing client for your firm in this capacity.

| **Example 1: wills and probate** |
|---|
| In the example of James Smith, the following points and consequences might have occurred to you:<br><br>1.  The deceased is the father of the client and therefore the relationship was close. It is particularly important for you to give your condolences and show empathy to the client.<br>2.  There is no will, so you need to consider the rules of intestacy.<br>3.  The deceased had a partner who lived with him, so there is the potential for a claim against the estate. You will need to gather information about the extent of the relationship. |

| **Example 2: property** |
|---|
| For Yusuf Ahmed's case, you might have thought of these points and consequences:<br><br>1.  This is a neighbour dispute, so there should be consideration given to whether a continuing relationship is important to the client.<br>2.  There is an ownership question and therefore you will want to consider:<br>     • Who currently owns the land, and is there a dispute?<br>     • If there is no dispute, whether the various parts of adverse possession can be made out:<br>          ○ time of occupation<br>          ○ actual occupation<br>          ○ intention to possess.<br>     • Will the neighbour oppose an application?<br>3.  The client wants to sell the property. You will need to ask specific questions to find out the client's main concerns. |

These are not comprehensive notes but they will be enough to remind you of the points that you must cover during the interview. Of course, every interview will be unique and individual issues will unfold and develop over the course of the discussion.

Having a clear structure in your mind as to how you want to proceed and which points to prioritise should help you to conduct a well-organised interview, thus achieving **AC 3** (see page x). A plan can be useful in an assessed interview situation where nerves can take hold or questioning goes differently to anticipated. Whether you write down a plan or retain it in your mind is a matter of personal preference (and might be down to the preparation time you have left) but, either way, having a plan should boost your confidence as you enter the interview.

### Assessment technique

If you do write down an interview plan, do not rush! Try to avoid a situation where you have quickly scrawled a plan and some valuable discussion points to raise in the interview but then need to spend time during the interview trying to decipher your own writing!

## ■ SUMMARY AND REFLECTION

It is almost inevitable that you might feel anxious ahead of the client interview assessment, but properly preparing ahead of the assessment and also planning how to get the most out of the ten-minute preparation time on assessment day should give you confidence and quell your nerves.

As we have discussed, preparing for the assessment and using your ten-minute preparation time wisely will give you the best chance of meeting the assessment criteria in the client interview:

- **AC 1** and **AC 2**: practising interview skills before the assessment will improve your listening and communicating skills.
- **AC 3**: planning will help you to conduct a well-organised interview.
- **AC 4**: by identifying the client's potential issue, you can begin to demonstrate client-focus.
- **AC 5**: careful preparation for the assessment will boost your confidence in your abilities and allow you to win your client's trust.

Thorough preparation will stand you in good stead for the beginning of the interview, to be discussed in the next chapter.

# 2

# The interview: part I

There are many different elements to an initial client interview. This book breaks them down into four stages:

1. Open the interview and develop a professional relationship.
2. Gather information from the client.
3. Provide advice (legal and non-legal).
4. Conclude the interview.

Different structures for a client interview are possible, and you might want to create your own individual approach and structure. However, for the SQE2 interview assessment, we recommend you follow the order outlined above as this will give your interview a logical and coherent structure. For example, it is illogical to offer advice before you have gathered all the information from the client. As such, it makes sense to gather all the relevant information from the client before you move on to give advice.

This chapter will focus on the first and second stages, and Chapter 3 will focus on the third and fourth stages. It is important to note that this does *not* mean that your time should be equally split between these stages but you should ensure that you cover all four stages before the interview is completed. Note that the SRA's sample interview on their website spends very little time on stage 1 and moves quickly to client questioning in stage 2. However, the guidance on stage 1 given below should help you to develop a professional relationship with the client (and thereby meet **AC 5**) and support you in later practice as a Day One Solicitor.

## ■ MAKING NOTES

Before we begin to explore different elements of the interview, we would like to emphasise the importance of taking notes. To give yourself the best chance of meeting the SQE2 attendance note assessment criteria (which will be explored in Chapter 4), you need to make notes of what is being said whilst the interview is taking place, right from the very beginning. The moment the client interview is over, your memory of what was said will start to fade. This can apply not only to the specific details but even to the general concepts. Everyone has a different memory capacity: you might think that you would be able to remember the key information after the interview ends but there is always a risk that you will forget important points, particularly under the stress of exam conditions.

There are drawbacks to taking notes during the interview as it will mean that you will inevitably lose eye contact with the client for some parts of the conversation. Clients will normally expect notes to be taken, but it would be a courtesy and a logical step in the process to anticipate any objections by explaining that you will be taking notes as you go along so that you have the clearest record of what they are saying and can better understand their situation.

Some points of guidance on taking notes during the interview:

- Do not write down what is said verbatim, as this will prevent you from properly listening to the client. Instead, note down the crucial points of your discussion.
- These notes will be useless to you if you cannot read them! When writing your attendance note, you cannot afford to waste time deciphering your handwriting, and working out whether the client has a problem with a cat or a rat, for example. Focus on making sure that what you write down is legible, and work on your handwriting if you can anticipate challenges here.
- Be aware of the need to maintain eye contact with the client in order to develop your rapport with them (as required by client interview **AC 3**). Do not be tempted to just look down at or read from your notes whilst you are talking.
- Making notes can be a good opportunity to control the pace of the interview. You have a limited amount of time, and the temptation will be to rush the client. But, if you are not able to write legibly as they talk, then you could ask them to slow down a little to ensure that you are able to record the information that they are giving to you. Not only will this help you to keep an accurate record but it also shows the client that you are listening and paying attention to them (**AC 1**), which will help to develop a positive rapport and demonstrate your competence (**AC 3**).

### Assessment technique

Practise taking notes with a peer or friend: see if you can improve your ability to write down key facts and build a timeline of key events and issues, whilst maintaining eye contact.

If you are used to typing your work on a keyboard, make sure that you practise writing notes by hand so that you feel comfortable and confident in the assessment.

## ■ STAGE 1: OPEN THE INTERVIEW AND DEVELOP A PROFESSIONAL RELATIONSHIP

The classic adage is that you only get one opportunity to make a first impression, and it is vital that you bear this in mind when deciding how to begin the interview with the client.

This is an opportunity for the client to get to know who you are and the role that you will play in their case, which may become, in time, one of the most important aspects of their life. It is also an opportunity for you to understand any of the emotions that the client might be feeling in this case, such as nerves, anger, frustration or fear.

In the SQE2 assessment the role is being played by the assessor and so none of this is real. However, in order to prove your competence according to the SRA's assessment criteria you need to engage with the fictional nature of this interview and behave appropriately, as if the assessor client really has suffered a bereavement or is frustrated by a neighbour dispute, for example.

### Interview technique

Try to view and treat the client in the SQE2 interview as if they were a real client. This will give the best possible opportunity of demonstrating your capacity to build a professional relationship with the client as required by **AC 3**: conduct yourself in a professional manner and treat the client with courtesy, respect and politeness, including respecting diversity where relevant.

The opening of the interview is also a chance for you to deal with any residual nerves that remain after your ten-minute preparation time. You cannot predict what the client will tell you or how they will respond to your questions and advice but you can anticipate and prepare for the opening section of the interview. This is therefore a golden opportunity for you to connect with the client, beginning the process of building the professional relationship with them, and to settle yourself so that you can give the best possible interview. See the SRA's performance indicators for **AC 3** in Appendix 1: building a rapport with your client is crucial to meeting this assessment criterion.

---

**Interview technique**

Do not rush the opening! In particular, try to take a deep breath before you start so that you have a clear, even pace when you begin talking. Being nervous might cause you to talk too quickly, so try to be aware of this and gauge from the client's reaction whether you need to adjust your approach and slow down. See the SRA's performance indicator for **AC 3**: you need to be 'well organised; calm, composed and efficient' and 'not appear rushed'.

---

This stage of the interview will be considered in two parts:

- The basics – including introductions and icebreakers.
- The formalities – covering professional conduct issues such as the duty of confidentiality.

## THE BASICS

### Introductions

Many candidates ask: 'How do I start an interview?' The best answer is also the simplest.

---

**Example 1: wills and probate**

An appropriate start to this interview might be:

> Hello, Mr Smith [or Good morning/Good afternoon/Good evening]. Thank you for making the time to come to our firm today. I am a solicitor at this firm.

---

You should note that on the example videos from the SRA the candidate does not refer to their name, and so simply stating that you are a solicitor will suffice by way of personal introduction. You are not expected to introduce yourself as your Candidate Number. If you are uncertain as to whether 'Good morning' or 'Good afternoon' should be used between 12.00 and 13.00, the neutral 'Hello' is always appropriate.

It is likely (if not inevitable) that the assessor will confirm that they are the person that you are expecting, and it is logical for you to follow up with:

> I understand you would like to discuss a property/wills and probate matter.

This might seem an obvious point, but being sure that you know the identity of the client and the subject of their enquiry will, by itself, give you a confidence boost and put you into a positive mindset for the upcoming interview.

In the assessment, it is likely that the client will already be seated, as you will be entering the room to them and not vice versa. In practice, you would politely ask the client to take a seat.

This is also a good opportunity to ask some courtesy questions. For example, you might want to clarify:

- how to pronounce their name if you are not familiar with it
- the client's preferred pronouns; it is important not to make assumptions
- whether they wish to be addressed by their first name or their surname with preferred title.

---

### Example 2: property

When meeting this client, to clarify this third point you might say:

> Hello, Mr Ahmed. Thank you for making the time to come here today. I am a solicitor at the firm. May I check if you would like me to call you Mr Ahmed or Yusuf?

---

### Interview technique: if in doubt, ASK!

These questions serve a dual purpose, both relating to **AC 3** for the SQE2 client interview assessment where you need to demonstrate your ability to conduct yourself in a professional manner and treat the client with courtesy and respect:

1. The questions will help you to remain confident, as one of the worst feelings in an interview is the worry that you are missing something or getting something wrong. If you spend even 0.1% of your brain capacity worrying about how to pronounce the client's name or what you should call them and causing possible offence, you will not be focusing all of your attention on the crucial aspects of the interview. It is much easier to resolve the issue immediately.
2. The questions demonstrate that you are taking care to check something that is very personal to the client. This small gesture is a good foundation for establishing a professional relationship, and a good reason for asking at least one of these questions even if you are confident of the answer.

## Breaking the ice

It is tempting to jump straight into the next stage of the opening, but remember that the client still does not know a great deal about you, and you need to 'break the ice': make the client feel at ease with you by asking some general questions or making general comments. You can choose your own phrasing but we recommend these two primary approaches.

### The formulaic approach

You could use a variety of generic icebreakers, ranging from comments about the weather or transport to questions on how the client is feeling. There is nothing fundamentally wrong with these examples, and they do demonstrate that you are focusing on the client and trying to build a relationship, but in practice be cautious as they can come across as trite, clichéd and tedious.

---

### Interview technique

One of the risks of using generic icebreakers is that because they have usually been heard so many times before they can be irritating to the client. This is the opposite reaction to the one you are hoping for!

Let's explore why some icebreakers might not be successful:

> Did you manage to find the office?

Of course they did, otherwise they would not be sitting in front of you!

> How was the traffic?

You are making an assumption that the client has driven/can drive. They might have walked, cycled or taken the train or tram.

> The weather is terrible, isn't it?

Very British, very neutral and completely irrelevant to the case.

> How are you doing today?

This is a genuine question about the client, which is a good start. The problem is that a person does not normally go to see a solicitor for the first time if things are going well. This therefore has the potential to be interpreted as a pointless question and might be particularly unsuitable in a wills and probate case. Also, as this is an open question, a talkative client might just start talking about the case before you have had the chance to cover other introductory points.

These icebreakers could be valuable in some contexts but you do need to be aware of their limitations. For the SQE2 client interview assessment, you might make a better impression on your client/assessor by following the second approach, explained below.

### The personal approach

A far better choice as an icebreaker is a personal question that relates either to the client themselves or to the problem that has brought them to your office in the first place. It speaks to the client directly but does not begin to explore their situation in great detail.

1.  **Relating to the client**

    - Try to connect with the client based on any initial indications of their personality or interests, particularly if it links to something that is of interest to you. For example, if they are wearing a football shirt, you could ask a question about their team's fortunes.
    - If you can see from their address in the documents that they might have had a difficult journey to get to your office, this can be a good starting point (note the difference between a personal discussion based on their actual journey and the generic 'How was the traffic?').

    A criticism of this approach is that an interview is a professional, not a social, meeting. However, clients are often nervous before a solicitor's meeting, and part of your job is to help them feel at ease so that they feel comfortable talking to you; this, in turn, enables you to gather all the information you need from the client. This is harder in the artificial assessment environment because the actor's attire may not connect to the client's personality, and the address will be fictitious. It is not always possible to use this type of icebreaker but just remember to show that you are making an effort to form rapport with the client, so that you are able to demonstrate **AC 3**.

## 2.  Relating to the case

The second type of personal icebreaker is to refer to something related to the case.

The wills and probate interview provides a straightforward way of doing this: as in **Example 1: wills and probate** on page xv, it is likely that someone has died and, because the client has come to see you about it, there is a strong chance that they were connected to that person. The obvious icebreaker is to offer your condolences for their loss. This is something that you would absolutely want to do anyway at some point, but by doing it early you can start to build the personal connection with the client, and segue into the professional interview. It is, however, also worth bearing in mind the slim chance that the client is not upset about the death! The email is likely to have given some information or indication of their relationship to the client.

This kind of connection is harder to achieve with the property interview, as you may not have sufficiently detailed information to allow you to ask a suitable question. However, when you read the email during the ten-minute preparation time, check to see if there is anything there that you can use as an icebreaker question: does the property have an unusual name, for example?

Unless there is an obvious comment to make or question to ask, be careful when using this approach. There is a risk that the client might immediately start to tell you about their situation, which will then throw your structure off course and potentially leave you discombobulated.

As you can see from the advice above, there may be situations in which an icebreaker is a helpful way of establishing a connection with the client. However, you should consider which, if any, are appropriate to the client you are interviewing. Do not worry too much about using an icebreaker but do remember they can be a useful tool to help put the client at ease when they first enter the interview room.

## THE FORMALITIES

In practice you would need to discuss certain client care issues with the client at this point. However, this is unnecessary for the SQE2 client interview assessment. In the SRA's online sample question for client interviewing, candidates are expressly told that they will not be assessed on 'client care matters (including costs) or money laundering issues'. Whilst 'client care matters' is a little vague, you will not need to discuss how much the interview will cost, contact details, your role in the firm, what the conflict of interest process is, the firm's policy on accepting cash, or whether acceptable identification has been received from the client. In practice, you would be expected to cover these points.

This does leave a number of areas that either should be covered in the introduction or may technically fall within the definition of 'client care matters' but you still need to think about how/when to include them. Many of them provide an opportunity to develop the professional relationship with the client, as you explain why they are important. For example, if you were asking for the client's contact details, you would emphasise the reasons: so that you can ensure that you can contact them with updates, and to empower the client by asking them to clarify which is their preferred method of communication.

There are two 'formalities' that in practice would usually be covered in stage 1 of the interview: the issue of confidentiality and the proposed structure of the interview.

## Confidentiality

Confidentiality is the bedrock of the client interview. With certain exceptions (such as suspected money laundering or terrorism activities), everything that the client tells you must be kept private and cannot be disclosed to anyone outside the firm without the client's express consent and authority. You are legally required to inform the client of this, as you owe your client a duty of confidentiality. Be aware that in the sample interviews that have been provided by the SRA this is not said by the candidate and therefore it appears that you will not have to mention it. However, the way in which you explain confidentiality to the client could help you to:

- settle the client's nerves, demonstrating a client-focused approach as required in **AC 4**
- embed the professional relationship and build their trust and confidence in you; this would be an opportunity to prove your competency in **AC 5**.

In practice, you would discharge your obligation in respect of confidentiality by a simple statement:

> Everything that you tell us during the course of this interview will be kept confidential. There are some rare instances in which we are required to disclose information to a third party, for example, money laundering or terrorism activities; however these exemptions to confidentiality are unlikely to arise in your case. I would therefore encourage you to answer my questions as fully as possible as this will enable me to get a good understanding of your issue(s) and offer you the most appropriate advice.

This achieves your objective and, most importantly, does so in language that is plain, accessible and easy to understand. This statement would protect you by making it clear that there are some exceptions to the principle of confidentiality, even if the chances are low that the exceptions will be triggered by the relevant SQE2 assessment topics.

After informing the client of their right to confidentiality, you should also clarify that the client understands the information that you have outlined to them. For example, you can say something like:

> I hope that I have clearly outlined the duty of confidentiality to you, but if you have any questions about it then please let me know.

This would allow you to gauge the client's understanding. When you practise interviews before the assessment, your interviewee's response should indicate whether you need to improve your communication skills here, in order to prove your competency in **AC 2**. This assessment criterion states that you must:

Communicate and explain in a way that is suitable for the client to understand.

This is covered in more detail in Chapter 3 when forming your advice for the client, but it is equally important, if not more so, in the early stages of the interview because this is when you are making a first impression. It is vital that you express yourself clearly and make sure that you use language that is not complicated and easy to understand.

Remember that the client has come to you for help but they do not know you and have no reason to trust you. A potential hurdle that you need to address is whether the client will trust you enough to tell you everything that you need to know, and whether they are motivated to be as helpful as they can in providing you with information. There is no single way of achieving this, but by emphasising the principle of confidentiality you are trying to create an atmosphere of trust and respect that is conducive to the client volunteering the information you need.

You should, therefore, think about what confidentiality can mean to the client. They might feel that the principle of confidentiality gives them the freedom to share information with you whether or not they trust you, because you have a duty not to disclose it. This is implicit in the statement above but you should always try to make sure that this kind of principle is as clear as possible for the client. You might therefore choose to reformulate and expand your explanation of the duty of confidentiality.

> It's important that I provide you with the best possible advice. In order to do this, it is important that I have a full and accurate understanding of your circumstances. Sometimes, the questions I ask may seem irrelevant or personal so, where possible, I will try to help you understand why I am asking you for this information. Also, everything you tell me will be confidential. This means that whatever you tell us cannot be passed on, outside this firm, without your permission. There are some rare instances in which we are required to disclose information to a third party, for example money laundering or terrorism activities; however, these exemptions to confidentiality are unlikely to arise in your case. I would therefore encourage you to answer my questions as fully as possible as this will enable me to get a good understanding of your issue(s) and offer you the most appropriate advice.

Although this explanation is longer than the one provided in the first example, it still uses accessible language rather than unnecessarily complex legal jargon. However, rather than being purely a statement of formality, this now reassures the client and addresses their possible concerns, which could motivate them to share more information with you; these are all part of building the professional relationship and trust with the client as required under **AC 5**. Communicating with the client in this way allows you to fulfil your legal obligation whilst also building your relationship with the client.

### Structure

It is also sensible to provide the client with an overview of the structure of the interview. How and when you choose to discuss this is entirely up to your personal taste, although for obvious reasons it should be fairly early in the assessment. One option is to be very precise and state exactly what issues will be discussed and the relevant order (this approach is more likely to be relevant for probate) and an alternative is to follow a more relaxed structure, as shown in the example below.

Discussing structure with the client brings two advantages. First, it allows the client – who may never have met a solicitor before and/or may be apprehensive about what to expect – to understand how the interview will be conducted. For the purposes of the SQE2 assessment, the interview is time-limited so you need to make sure you can stick to a clear structure. Outlining that to the client briefly at the outset will enable you to control the interview, a competency listed under **AC 3**.

So, you could say:

> We have 25 minutes for this meeting and in a moment I will begin by asking you how I can help you and why you have made an appointment with us today. I'll spend some time asking further questions to build a clearer picture of your circumstances, and will then summarise to make sure that I have a complete understanding of the situation. Then I will explain the legal position to you, and provide some preliminary advice to help you understand where you stand in this case and how you can practically move forward. If you want to ask questions at any point, please do ask.

The second advantage of setting the structure out at an early stage is that it manages the expectations of the client, which is a competency under **AC 5** as part of establishing and maintaining an effective relationship with the client. It is usual for a client to ask for legal advice at various points throughout an interview, often at an early stage and before you have gathered all of the information that you need in order to be able to answer the question completely. If you do not clarify that the advice will come later in the interview, you will be torn between not being able to answer their question (and having to explain why) and answering their question without having all of the necessary information, potentially undermining your position and authority. Setting the structure does not mean that the client will not ask for advice early on but if they do so, it will be much easier to explain why you cannot answer immediately as you have already set the expectation that the advice will follow later.

### Interview technique

Try to put yourself in the position of a nervous client who does not know what to expect from this initial interview. If you were seeking legal advice, think about how you would like to be treated and spoken to by the solicitor. This should help you to appreciate how the client in your interview might be feeling.

## ■ STAGE 2: GATHER INFORMATION FROM THE CLIENT

A primary aim of an initial client interview is to gather information from the client to enable you to understand their legal issue and their needs, aims and objectives so that you can provide preliminary advice. Although we have devoted many pages to approaching stage 1, the introductions in your SQE2 interview assessment will be dealt with quite quickly, and you will soon find yourself at the stage of gathering information. This is the critical part of the assessment as client care and legal advice are not technically assessed or required to pass the assessment.

This section will look at:

- why you need to gather information
- how to gather information
- specific areas of focus for wills and probate
- specific areas of focus for property.

When you have finished gathering information, it will be helpful for you to summarise it to your client. Some guidance is provided at the end of this chapter on how best to achieve this.

## PURPOSE OF GATHERING INFORMATION

You might think that the most important part of the initial client interview is providing advice to the client. Whilst this is certainly important, and is the focus of Chapter 3, information-gathering is also a vital part of the interview. In fact, if you do not gather all of the relevant information, you will probably not be able to offer correct or suitable advice. Remember that the advice you give in the SQE2 assessment is preliminary advice only, and the accuracy of the advice does not impact whether you pass or fail the assessment. In practice it is often necessary to undertake research, gather further information or review documents before being able to offer further advice.

It might help you to think about the information-gathering part of the interview using this analogy: when you enter the client interview you are, effectively, walking into a room that is almost completely dark. You can see very little of your surroundings. There are brief streaks of light that illuminate the surroundings a little, representing the information provided by the memorandum that you reviewed in the ten-minute preparation period. There is, however, nowhere near enough light to see the path that allows you safe passage to the door on the other side of the room, which signals the end of the interview. If you attempt to walk that path and form your advice for the client in this limited light, you will probably fall prey to the numerous obstacles that exist along the way but that you cannot see.

| Example 2: property |
|---|
| After reading about Yusuf Ahmed's case, any number of possibilities could occur to you. If you pick one and focus on it without considering anything else, then you are gambling on your assumptions being correct. For example, you might assume that claiming the land is the most important aspect of this case for your client. Unless you explore the client's concerns more widely, this could lead you to give advice that is not client-focused and therefore does not meet **AC 4**. |

The good news is that you have it within your power to summon more light into this darkened room! The client can provide additional light – ie information – to enable you to find a safe path. Your job is to utilise the tools in your kit to gain access to this light/ information and thus increase the likelihood that you provide accurate advice to the client and exit the room safely. The primary way of doing this is to ask questions!

## METHODS OF GATHERING INFORMATION

Remember that **AC 1** for SQE2 client interviewing is dedicated to (1) listening to your client and (2) asking questions:

> Listen to the client and use questioning effectively to enable the client to tell the solicitor what is important to them.

### Listening skills

The SRA's performance indicators for this assessment criterion state:

> The candidate demonstrates active listening skills and engagement with the client, for example by
> 1. listening attentively (use of facial expressions/body language/tone of voice/ may evidence this)
> 2. avoiding interrupting the client
> 3. listening without judgement
> 4. avoiding making assumptions.

Your listening skills are relevant throughout the whole interview: you must show that you are actively listening to the client and understand the points that they are making. This requirement will be noted at various points below as we move through the interview stages, but first let's look more closely at how you can demonstrate your competence in these performance indicators.

### Listen attentively

Whilst the client is talking, make sure that they know that you are listening closely and attentively. You can achieve this by using non-verbal techniques, such as:

- nodding your head
- keeping good eye contact with the client
- having an open body language – do not sit back with your arms folded, as this can seem aggressive, hostile or impatient
- making notes in response to what they say
- adapting your tone of voice if your client is divulging personal or upsetting information
- generally engaging with the client – focus on them and do not appear distracted.

These techniques should be used in good measure: clearly you do not need to be constantly nodding your head but some visual indication that you are listening whilst the client is speaking will foster an atmosphere of trust and confidence, and thereby help you to achieve **AC 5** in the assessment.

### Avoid interrupting the client

There are very few situations in which you should interrupt your client. Under time pressure in the SQE2 assessment you may be tempted to interrupt them in order to make sure that you complete the interview in the allotted time. However, by interrupting the client you are sending the message that you are not interested in them, and that you are not listening properly.

There are rare occasions when interrupting might be necessary. If the client is giving you a lot of information about the case and you are struggling to follow everything, you might want to interrupt in order to check what has been said. If you must interrupt the client, then make sure you do so courteously, and always explain why you have done so.

---

**Example 2: property**

Yusuf might speak about a dispute with someone without saying who that person is. If that happened, you could say:

> Yusuf, I apologise for interrupting. I do want you to continue but, before you do, can I just check who this person is?

This approach allows your client to answer the question and clarify the crucial information before returning to the discussion.

---

If possible, wait until the client has finished speaking, and then you can summarise what has been said to clarify anything that has been missed. You will see at the end of this chapter that we advise you to summarise the client's information once the questioning is complete but it can also be useful to summarise at earlier stages, particularly if the client has told you a lot of information and you need to confirm that you have heard and understood everything that has been said. Be mindful that you do not overuse this technique, however: if you summarise every time that your client says something, it will have the opposite effect and suggest that you were not listening closely enough the first time.

*Listen without judgement*

You need to gain the client's trust and confidence to encourage them to divulge personal information so that you can build a full picture of the case. If the client feels that you are making value judgements on their behaviour or actions, they will feel uncomfortable and less likely to share vital information with you. Try to adopt a neutral facial expression and do not react emotionally to anything the client tells you.

*Avoid making assumptions*

This part of the interview is a vital time for you to hear the client's perspective on the matter. If you listen carefully to the client, you should be able to understand their goals and what they want to achieve by coming to see you. However, if you assume that you already know which path they might want to take and do not listen properly to what they are telling you, this will be damaging to your professional relationship and might lead you later in the interview to give advice that is inappropriate for their circumstances. Remember to keep an open mind and be prepared to balance legal and non-legal options as being in the best interests of the client (this is explored further on page 49).

## Questioning skills

A good synonym for the client *interviewing* assessment would be a client *questioning* assessment, as this reflects the primary method that you have of gathering information. In fact, when you are interviewing a client and you find that you run out of things to say, asking a question is always a good way to get you back on track and bring a new direction to your conversation. It is important to stress, however, that the questions you ask must serve a purpose and, where possible, should be asked in a coherent and logical order.

There are different types of questions and they each have different purposes: open, closed and leading questions.

For this assessment you will primarily need to ask open and closed questions. There is a technical difference between them. Be reassured that the SQE2 client/assessor is not going to ask you to label or describe your question but it is important for you to understand the difference between the two types of question and the types of situation in which to use them.

**Open questions** require the client to provide more than a one-word response (such as 'yes' or 'no'). They ask the client to provide information of some form and are, therefore, often prefaced by words such as 'how', 'what', 'why', 'where' and 'who'. For example:

How did that happen?

What happened next?

Why do you think that happened?

Where did this take place?

Who else knew about this?

If you posed these questions to the client, it is clear that the answer would be entirely their own. They could not be guided by your questions to give a particular answer, as they might with a leading question (see below).

**Closed questions** are in stark contrast to open questions. You are directing the client towards a particular answer, and most closed questions can be answered with a simple 'yes' or 'no', or a very short answer. For example, in the property interview you might ask:

> Do you own the property?

> Do you live alone?

> Do you own the property alone?

If these questions were posed to the client, they could only use a limited range of answers. For the first two questions the answer has to be 'yes' or 'no'. For the third question, the only answers that make sense are 'yes' or 'no, with someone else'.

The two types of question can therefore produce very different types of answers from the client, and they are both valuable. However, much like one torch that provides a wide beam and another that generates a narrow, focused light, open and closed questions should be deployed in different ways at different times. Let's assess the respective merits of both types of question.

### Advantages of open questions

As shown earlier, open questions allow the client to give the answer that is most natural to them, without the interviewer placing limitations on that answer. Open questions allow the client to:

- set out their perspective and understanding of the situation, in as much detail as they choose
- express their emotions and thoughts or concerns about the situation, which might lead you to understand why they performed a particular action or feel a particular way about the case.

### Disadvantages of open questions

The drawback of open questions is, essentially, a mirror image of their merits. The lack of direction for the client means that they might not know where to start or finish explaining their issue, and as the SQE2 assessment is limited by time it is very easy for the interview to lose structure. A natural but unfocused first question of 'How can I help you today?' or 'What has brought you here today?' can lead to a client not understanding what information you are looking for and talking incessantly about information that is at best tangential and at worst completely irrelevant. Neither of these situations is conducive to a clear and effective interview, a performance indicator under **AC 3**: 'the candidate maintains control of the interview'.

Put simply, open questions encourage the client to provide information to the interviewer.

*Advantages of closed questions*

By contrast, the main advantage of closed questions is that the interviewer is in control of the questioning. If you want to ask about a very narrow topic, for example the impact of a particular person on the client's property issue or about the relatives of a particular person, you can just ask a closed question that narrows the scope to that issue.

---

### Example 2: property

In this interview, you could ask the following closed questions:

> Yusuf, when did you purchase the property?

> Has your neighbour objected to you using the land?

> Is your property on the market?

Yusuf is going to answer the first question with a date and the other two questions with 'yes', 'no', 'I don't know' or a specific answer, likely to be only one or two words long. After gaining this information, you can ask follow-up questions.

---

Inevitably, then, closed questions are perfect tools for focusing on a particular issue and obtaining specific details. They can also help the client to understand what you are looking for, rather than having to guess, which may be the case with an open question that is not clearly presented.

*Disadvantages of closed questions*

Much like open questions, the weakness of closed questions is closely aligned to their strength. Because they have a narrow focus, if used in isolation there is a risk that the wider issues of the situation will not be explored, and the conversation will be on what *you* want to talk about and not what *the client* wants to talk about. Closed questions do not allow the client to provide anything but very short answers and, to return to our previous metaphor of the interview as a dark room, they can only add a small amount of light.

Closed questions are unhelpful in determining how the client feels about the issue, which you need to understand in order to demonstrate a client-focused approach and see the problem from the client's point of view, as required by **AC 4**. A closed question will also never generate an independent and uninfluenced answer from the client.

*Conclusion*

This assessment of open and closed questions leads us to the obvious conclusion that you should aim to utilise both types in your SQE2 client interview assessment, as specified in **AC 1**. As with any communication, there is no right or wrong time to ask each of these, but below we explore two strategies for structuring your questions.

## The funnel approach

A good way of approaching questions is to use what is commonly called the funnel approach (see Figure 2.1). This is based around the design of a funnel, which has a wide opening at the top before narrowing down so that the contents can be poured into a smaller receptacle.

Applying this to questioning:

- Begin with open questions to get a broad perspective and understanding of the overall situation.
- Respond to the answers that you have been given by probing for additional, related information.
- Then ask closed questions in order to narrow down the focus of the interview and acquire specific information or details relevant to the client's case.

This does not mean that you should avoid open questions later on, and you might need to revert to open questions in order to gain a better understanding of a particular issue. It is important that you use your judgement to decide what questions are suitable in any given situation.

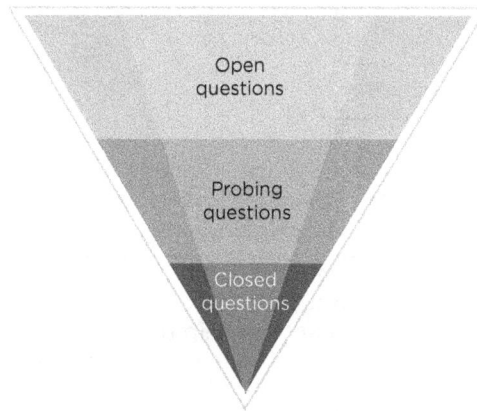

*Figure 2.1: The funnel approach to questioning*

---

### Example 2: property

Following the funnel approach, you might form the following questions:

> Yusuf, why is this additional land important to you? [*Open question*]

> What would it mean to you if you didn't own this land? [*Open/probing question*]

> Is the property on the market? [*Closed question*]

> How much is it being advertised for? [*Closed question*]

> What would the value of the property be if you did not have this land? [*Closed question*]

The purpose of the first two questions is to give you a broad understanding of Yusuf's situation and allow you to select the most appropriate closed questions to follow up with. Here, Yusuf might answer that the land is important to him because he wants to sell it and maximise its value, and that if he did not own the land the value of the property would be lower. These answers tell you that you need to find out the specific monetary values of the land or property, which should then be revealed when the client answers the three closed questions shown here.

## Responding to your client

We noted earlier that open questions invite the client to talk, whilst closed questions draw out shorter answers. You can therefore also use the different types of question depending on the extent to which the client is prepared to talk without significant prompting. For example:

- You might only need to ask a few open questions to a client who is keen to talk and happy to respond, but you might need to deploy closed questions to keep them on track and avoid straying beyond the most relevant aspects of the interview.
- By contrast, a client who is reluctant to talk may not respond well to open questions at an early stage of the interview. You might need to ask closed questions to draw them out of their shell, before then moving to open questions.

### Example 1: wills and probate

Using a combination of open and closed questions could result in the following dialogue with the client in this case:

Candidate:  James, can you help me to understand the situation that has brought you here today? [*Open question, to provide an overview of the situation*]

James:  My father has died.

Candidate:  I am very sorry to hear that. Please accept my condolences. May I ask what in particular you would like my help with? [*Open question*]

James:  To deal with it.

Candidate:  I see. I need to ask some questions that might be sensitive, but it is important for me to understand the situation more fully. I understand that your father's name was Simon; is that correct? [*Closed question*]

James:  Yes.

Candidate:  Thank you. I understand from what I have been told that there was no will? [*Closed question*]

James:  That's right.

The initial open questions did not yield much information, so the candidate has pivoted to closed questions. Once they have gleaned some additional information, they could then move back to open questions.

## Asking questions linked to documents

A final note on using open and closed questions is to remind you to make use of any documents that have been provided in the ten-minute preparation window before the interview. Asking questions based on these documents can help you to gain a much clearer understanding of the issue, particularly if you are someone who prefers to receive information visually.

The SQE2 assessment for the wills and probate interview might provide you with a will as an additional document. It is likely that the client will have a copy as well, although you should check this. When asking relevant open or closed questions about the will, it would be useful for you to refer to specific parts of the document and take the client through it, checking that they understand the issue. This allows you to ensure that you are dealing with each point on an issue-by-issue basis and also helps to communicate to the client that you are fully in control of the situation and are managing the interview appropriately.

| Example 1: wills and probate |
|---|
| In the event that there is no will, as in the James Smith case, there may still be additional documents to review, by way of letters or death certificates. |

This technique is even more useful in the SQE2 property interview assessment. You might receive a plan and have already gleaned some useful information from it, but if you have asked open questions so that the client can describe something, such as the extent of land that they wish to claim adverse possession over, do not be afraid to ask them to sketch their understanding of that extent of land on the plan. You can also point to specific parts of the document and ask questions. The document can help to provide context and give you a much clearer picture of what the client is talking about.

| Example 2: property |
|---|
| Having listened to Yusuf's explanation of the situation, you might follow up with: |

> Yusuf, thank you for explaining the land. Would you be able to do a quick sketch on this piece of paper for me, to make it as clear as possible?

A diagram or plan might not always be necessary, but in any situation where there are boundary disputes it is always useful to get even a rough sketch so that you have a better visual idea of the land. In this scenario, Yusuf's plan might look like the diagram in Figure 2.2:

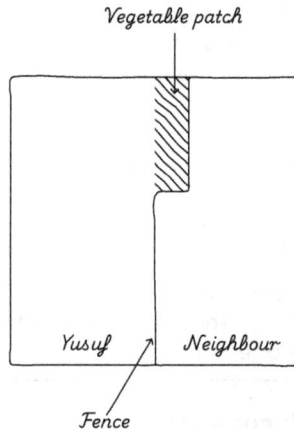

Figure 2.2: An example of a client sketch

## Leading questions

Leading questions are commonly used by advocates when conducting cross-examinations of hostile witnesses or witnesses who are presenting evidence contrary to the advocate's case. This should give you an indication of their value when talking to your own client in the SQE2 assessment – ie, they should be avoided. Put simply, leading questions are those where you put an answer into the question, thus leading the individual towards that answer. For example:

> You hold this property as joint tenants, don't you?

You might need to obtain this important information. However, it is a leading question because it suggests the answer to the client. They may answer 'yes' or they may answer 'no' but their answer provides little value because you have guided or even pushed them into giving it. By contrast, you could follow this approach:

> Do you know how the ownership of the property between you and [X] was set out?

If this open question fails – and as the client is unlikely to have knowledge of property law, it probably will fail – then you can move to a closed question:

> There are two ways you can co-own property: joint tenants, and tenants in common. Do you know which it was?

This is a closed question because you are providing the possible answers. However, you are not guiding the client towards one answer or the other, and so the information that you receive will be significantly more helpful.

It is difficult to envisage a situation where a leading question would be preferable to either an open question or a closed question, and therefore you should avoid them. Such questions can make a client feel pressured to answer in a particular way and they do not encourage open dialogue. This makes it difficult for the client to 'tell the solicitor what is important to them' (**AC 1**).

## WILLS AND PROBATE: LIKELY TOPICS

It is likely that the SQE2 wills and probate interview assessment will require you to advise a client on the consequences that flow from an individual's death. Some important information may be contained in the memorandum and any accompanying documentation (eg you may be able to determine that a will is valid). There will, however, be a lot of detailed information that will not be available from the documents and so you will need to gain it from the client.

A good starting point is to gather information on relevant topics that will help you to formulate further lines of questioning and may inform your advice. You might need to ask questions based on the following topics:

- relevant family history
- assets
- liabilities
- the client's expectations and goals.

These are all important for different reasons and, depending on the situation, will need a greater or lesser portion of your time in the interview assessment.

### Relevant family history

The main reason that you need to find out about the family of the deceased is that they will have a direct impact on the advice that you will be providing to the client. People may have a potential claim against the estate in respect of the will if they have not been provided for, and knowing whether anyone is in this category will help you to understand the scope of advice that will be needed later on in the interview.

It is also important to identify the status of individuals, as this will affect your advice. For example:

- The age of any children will affect bequests.
- Whether or not all of the beneficiaries are still living will affect the estate.

Knowing the family history is very important if the deceased has died intestate, as the rules of intestacy require an understanding of the immediate family tree to enable you to work out who will inherit the estate. For example, you will need to find out whether the deceased was married or in a civil partnership, and whether or not they had children.

From reading the will you should be able to identify the relevant people that you need to find out about, but do remember that this is a delicate situation and you need to be diplomatic and careful about how you phrase your enquiries. Questions such as 'Have you spoken to the executors?' or 'Do you know if they would be prepared to act as executors?' can help tease out information from the client.

## Assets

You will need to ask the client about their understanding of the available assets in the estate. An open question might secure this information but closed questions might be necessary so think ahead about how you can break down your enquiry to a series of narrower questions. Think about the different categories of assets, such as:

- property
- stocks and shares
- bank accounts
- individual valuable items
- pensions
- insurance policies.

Asking about each of these categories with a closed question should give you sufficient understanding of the estate's assets.

---

### Example 1: wills and probate

At this point, you could ask James the following closed questions:

Did Simon own any property?

Did he own any stocks or shares?

If the answers to these questions are 'yes', then you can ask further, specific closed questions.

---

It is also important to ask about details at this stage. For example:

- If there is a property or bank account, was it jointly owned or was Simon the sole owner?

- If the property was owned jointly, how was it held in equity? There is a significant difference between a property that is held as joint tenants and one that is held as tenants in equity. (See **Revise SQE: Trusts** to revise this topic.)
- What is the property worth? What are the shares worth? You might only get an approximate valuation at this stage (the client is unlikely to have an up-to-date property valuation or the instant valuation of shares); however, the client is likely to ask whether there will be any tax implications, and the only way that you can adequately answer this is by knowing approximately how much money is in the estate.

When going through the assets with the client, keep an eye on the will, if one exists. If there are items listed in the will that are not mentioned by the client, make sure to ask about them: either the client has forgotten about the items, in which case you can simply ask the client about them, or the items are no longer present, in which case you will have to form an opinion about their legal position.

If you are dealing with an intestacy situation then the questions are just as valid because of the tax implications. Inheritance tax is equally applicable to both wills and intestacy, so you will need to get a broad understanding, at least, of the value of the estate.

## Liabilities

We recommend that you take the same approach with liabilities as you did with the assets. Think about categories of debts, for example:

- funeral expenses
- monthly payments
- loans
- mortgages.

Use closed questions to ask the client about each category, and then ask an open question ('Are there any other debts?') to find out if there is anything that you have missed.

This is also a good time to ask whether the client is aware of any gifts that the deceased may have given away in the past seven years, which will have consequences when it comes to advice on tax liability.

## Client's goals and expectations

Finally, make sure you find out what the client's goals and expectations are in respect of this meeting. This is normally the last stage of information-gathering and it will help you to understand why they have come to see you and if there is a particular point that you need to focus on for advice. You need to:

- understand what the client wants to achieve
- avoid making assumptions
- think about practical considerations such as time and cost
- consider the client's relationship with other people involved in the matter.

Always bear in mind **AC 4**: to prove your competency, you need to show that you can focus on the client's specific issue and also understand their personal perspective on the matter.

## PROPERTY – LIKELY TOPICS

Property is a very broad topic but at least we can safely say that this assessment will be about land! We recommend breaking your questions down into the following categories, which are discussed in more detail below:

- the general background to the case
- the land and associated documents
- the client's status and other parties involved
- the client's goals and expectations.

## General background

Asking questions about the general background to the client's issue is a logical place to start, because this will help you to understand what the interview is about. You should have gained a brief understanding of the matter from the email in your ten-minute preparation time, and so you might not spend too much time on this, but it is a good opportunity to gain clarity and ask the client to explain the matter in their own words so that you can fully appreciate the crucial points.

Open questions will normally be best here because they enable you to get the client's perspective. You can follow up with closed questions if appropriate to get a more focused understanding.

## The land and associated documents

The next logical line of enquiry is about the land and any accompanying documents, because then you can get a clear picture of what the land is, who owns it and where the problems arise. You will need to refer to the documents for context, and here the questions are more likely to be closed than open because you will be referring to specific areas that you can identify as crucial to the matter but that the client might not.

For example: if the problem relates to a boundary dispute, your focus will probably be on steps that were taken to communicate *before* the actions were taken, whilst the client might want to talk about what happened *after* the actions. You will know that, in order to demonstrate that the criteria for adverse possession has been made out, the focus is on the 10 or 12 years preceding the claim. The client may well be focused on the recent events, which are less likely to be relevant to their legal position.

## The client's status and other parties involved

Once you have established a clear understanding of the land, the next step for information-gathering is the client themselves. This is your chance to flesh out information such as the client's legal entitlement to their land and how the situation has impacted upon them. You can ask questions that might be incidental to the specific topic of the interview but will be relevant when forming your advice, particularly as the advice will, by definition, be broader than in the wills and probate interview. For example, you will be able to gain a clearer understanding of the client and the other parties by asking open questions about:

- their history with the neighbour
- their thoughts about the property
- whether they have had problems in the past
- their plans for the future.

## The client's goals and expectations

Finally, as with the wills and probate interview, end the information-gathering stage by gaining a clear understanding of what the client wants to achieve and why that is. Again, open questions are the best approach here, so use them to prove your competency under **AC 4**.

## SUMMARISE THE KEY INFORMATION YOU HAVE GATHERED

Once you have gathered the relevant information from the client, it is time to move to the second part of the interview, forming the advice, which is explored in Chapter 3. However, there is one final, useful task that you should perform at this stage, and that is to summarise the information back to the client.

This is an important phase of the interview for three reasons: building a chronology/timeline, adding new information or correcting errors, and developing a professional relationship with the client.

### Build a chronology/timeline

Your goal is to gain as much relevant information as possible. By providing a summary of the information that you have received, you will be able to note any holes that exist in the chronology or in the information, and address them with follow-up questions. This is your last chance in the SQE2 assessment to prove your competency under **AC 1**, to use questioning effectively so that the client can communicate what is important to them.

---

**Example 2: property**

By the time you have finished asking questions to Yusuf, you may have gathered enough information to create the following chronology or timeline:

| | |
|---|---|
| June 2009 | Yusuf purchases property (registered land). Neighbour already owns their property (registered land) at this point. |
| May 2010 | Yusuf begins to use the area of land as a vegetable patch to grow potatoes and onions. |
| February 2025 | Yusuf decides to sell the property. |
| April 2025 | Yusuf places the property on the market. |
| 1 May 2025 | Yusuf receives an offer of £200,000 for the property. |
| 5 May 2025 | Klara (neighbour) demands that he stop using the land. |

This is a clear timeline. Creating a chronology of events will help you to formulate your thoughts clearly when you come to write the attendance note for this interview.

A timeline also allows you to fill in any gaps. If you had not written down the date in your chronology of when Yusuf starting to use the land, and you know that the matter involves adverse possession, it would be immediately apparent to you that there is a gap in your information.

---

### Add new information or correct errors

The summary also provides the client with a final opportunity to add any new information or correct information that they have provided erroneously. This can happen both under assessment conditions and in practice, and summarising is an opportunity to ensure that the information upon which you base your advice is accurate and, as far as is possible, complete.

---

**Interview technique**

Whilst giving your summary of the information to the client, ask yourself whether there is any missing information. For example, if you say, 'In June you were contacted by an agent', you might want to pause and ask for the precise date of this contact.

This is also an opportunity to clarify information provided by the initial questions, so you could also ask, 'How did the agent contact you in June?'

## Develop the professional relationship

The summary is important for the development of the professional relationship, an essential part of the SQE2 assessment as detailed in **AC 5**. In practice, an initial client interview is one amongst many similar interviews/assessments that a solicitor might complete in a day, but for the client this interview might be the most important event of their life. At this point of the SQE2 assessment, summarising what you have been told demonstrates that you have listened closely and sympathetically to the client, gained a good understanding of their case and understood the relevance of the personal information they have shared with you. This might be the first time that the client has discussed the issue with someone else, and having you summarise the matter to them reinforces your engagement with their case and with them.

### Assessment technique

Some tips to follow when summarising the information to the client:

1.  Do not simply repeat everything the client has said. The client has spent 10 to 15 minutes explaining the sequence of events to you and you do not have the same amount of time to repeat it back, nor would they be interested in that.
2.  Spend around a minute identifying the crucial points of the case and joining the dots between them. For example, in a wills and probate case you might identify:
    *   the deceased
    *   their relation to the client
    *   the brief contents of the will
    *   the key concerns of the client
    *   what the client hopes to achieve from this the meeting.
    These key points will form the basis of your advice to the client, stage 3 in our interview process, so make sure they are clear in your mind.
    As well as presenting the key information back to the client, this is a useful way of showing the assessor that you have gained a good overview of the events that have led to the client coming to see you. Bear in mind that the client is your assessor and so you are not only interviewing them but also signalling your understanding of the assessment criteria to them.
3.  Do not lend undue weight to particular facts simply because the client believes they are important or because they support the client's case. The client will be listening closely, and if you begin to imply that they have a very strong case by accentuating certain facts to make the client confident, then that will make it harder for them to understand if you tell them later in the interview that they have a weak case.
4.  This is when you will be able to see the knock-on effect of not listening carefully to the client or taking down incorrect facts during your information-gathering. You might have written down the incorrect name or made a miscalculation and, although this summary is a good chance to clarify the information, the client will interrupt the flow of your summary to correct any errors, which might unsettle you and knock your confidence. Be prepared for your client to intervene, and move quickly to correct errors so that you can maintain control of the interview and show that you are wholly focused on the client and their case.

5. Remember that after you have conducted the interview you will be writing an attendance note as the final part of the SQE2 assessment. Having a clear summary that the client agrees to will enable you to be confident that you can base your attendance note on a detailed and accurate factual history.

## ■ SUMMARY AND REFLECTION

By this point, opening the interview and gathering information should have provided you with ample opportunities to demonstrate your competency as indicated by the SQE2 assessment criteria, such as:

- **AC 1**: ask closed and open questions to gain a full picture of the client's case.
- **AC 1**: listen carefully and closely to the client.
- **AC 3**: build a professional relationship with the client through sensitive questioning and calm organisation.
- **AC 4**: focus on the client and their issue, and understand their views of the matter.
- **AC 5**: build the client's trust in your ability to understand the issue and take the matter further.

You should have developed a rapport with the client by now, and have a full and accurate understanding of the situation that they find themselves in. For our worked examples, you should have reached these stages:

- **Example 1: wills and probate** – you should have expressed your condolences to James and discovered significant information about the size of the estate, the extent of the family and the potential for claims against the estate.
- **Example 2: property** – you should have discovered the key claim that Yusuf wishes to raise and understood why it is important to him.

In short, you are ready to move on to the part that many candidates dread: advising the client on what to do next!

# 3

# The interview: part II

In Chapter 2 we introduced a possible four-stage structure to follow during your SQE2 client interview assessment:

1. Open the interview and develop a professional relationship.
2. Gather information from the client.
3. Provide advice (legal and non-legal).
4. Conclude the interview.

Chapter 2 considered stages 1 and 2 – how to begin the interview with a client in a legal matter, and the skills you will need to use to gather information. By the time you reach the end of stage 2, you should have a clear understanding of the situation that the client faces and be able to turn to stages 3 and 4: provide advice (legal and non-legal) and conclude the interview.

> ## Interview technique
> Do not worry about whether or not you have gathered every single piece of background information from the client during stage 2. This is rarely achieved, and as long as you have the central facts of the case you should be able to start formulating some legal advice.

This chapter considers stages 3 and 4 of the interview. Again, it is important to stress that there is no guidance for timing on each of these stages but you should spend longer on stages 2 and 3 than on stages 1 and 4. We will draw on **Example 1: wills and probate** and **Example 2: property** as set out in the introduction to add context to the techniques being discussed and show how you can demonstrate that you meet the SQE2 assessment criteria for client interviewing.

## ■ STAGE 3: PROVIDE ADVICE (LEGAL AND NON-LEGAL)

This is often the part of an interview that causes the most anxiety for SQE2 candidates. There are different reasons for this but the overriding concern is: pressure. Before this stage in the interview, most discussions can be planned and prepared, to a point, following a structure of asking open and closed questions to gather information about the client and their issue. Providing legal advice to the client, however, is much more difficult to plan for. You need to apply the client's specific situation to legal principles and form an opinion that will be the foundation for your legal and non-legal (practical) advice (which in real life the client would be paying money for – which brings added pressure!). Forming your opinion can be daunting, as you try to balance the facts before you: is the estate subject to inheritance tax or not? Does the client have a claim for adverse possession? Furthermore, you will be under the pressure of time in the SQE2 assessment and will, therefore, have to think quickly to reach a decision about what advice to offer.

We discussed how to deal with nerves in Chapter 1, and everyone will have their own way of dealing with the stress of the assessment environment. However, the assessment technique box below offers some general tips that might be useful and reassuring for you.

---

### Assessment technique

1. By summarising the information that you received from the client (as explored at the end of Chapter 2), you have given yourself some time to reflect on the key aspects which will form the basis of your advice. You might also have identified some relevant points during the questioning period. Note these down when you can so that you have a sound basis for your advice.

2. You are being asked to provide preliminary advice so it is perfectly appropriate to explain that this is initial advice and that a full written advice letter will follow. If you are unsure about a particular point in your SQE2 client interview assessment, there is nothing wrong with telling the client that you will check the precise rule and confirm the situation in writing.

3. Be confident! If you lack confidence in your advice, the client will have little confidence in your judgement and you will thereby fail to demonstrate competency in **AC 5**. Try to strike the right balance: do not be overconfident but avoid sounding hesitant and unsure of yourself. Repeating the same points or becoming flustered can reduce succinct advice to a long-drawn-out and confusing statement, and you won't achieve the performance indicators in **AC 3** (be well organised, calm, composed and efficient). These phrases might be helpful to include:

> There are arguments for both sides but based on what you have told me it appears that you do have a potential claim.

> The law is [x, y and z]. You have satisfied [*points x and y*], but [*point z*] will require more investigation.

4. When approaching this part of the client interview assessment, do bear in mind that the SQE2 assessment criteria focuses heavily on the general conduct of the *entire* interview. Try not to put yourself under too much pressure when forming your advice – although this is still significant, it is not the only important part of the interview. The accuracy of your advice is not being assessed, and the manner in which you deliver the advice is as important as the advice itself.

---

You will often have to multitask during this part of the interview: form your view on the client's legal position and the options available to them and then communicate this information to the client in a manner they can understand (**AC 2**).

As you analyse the information acquired during questioning (stage 2) to formulate your advice, we recommend structuring this part of the interview around the following action points:

- Assess the client's objectives and the needs arising from the situation.
- Analyse the client's legal matter.
- Provide the advice:
  - the legal aspects
  - the non-legal (practical) aspects.
- Outline the next steps.

Let's explore these actions in more detail.

## ASSESS THE CLIENT'S OBJECTIVES AND NEEDS

Before you reach stage 3 and begin to advise the client, it is imperative that during stage 2 you discovered what they are seeking to achieve. This will affect the direction of your legal advice but also the practical options that you choose to offer. As mentioned in Chapter 2, you can normally do this by a simple open question during the first half of the interview, such as:

> What are you hoping to achieve from this meeting?

> What resolution are you hoping to achieve?

> What is your primary aim moving forward?

You should also have understood the client's needs by obtaining sufficient information during stage 2, so that you can now provide sound advice. Some aspects of the situation can be quickly clarified; for example, if there is a will, is it valid? If there is property involved, who owns it? Other matters will unfold as you gain a better understanding of what the situation requires; for example, in a claim for adverse possession, you need to know for how long the squatter has occupied the land.

Let's explore the key information you might have gained so far from **Example 1** and **Example 2** (remind yourself of the details of each case on page xv).

---

### Example 1: wills and probate

During your ten-minute preparation time before the client interview began, you realised that you needed to establish:

- whether both James and Lucy are over the age of 18 and are therefore not minors
- whether Simon has other children or dependants likely to make a claim on his estate
- how long Simon has been living with Angela, so that you can advise on a potential claim by Angela under the Inheritance (Provision for Family and Dependants Act) 1975.

In order to continue using this worked example, let's say that you obtained the following facts during the information gathering in stage 2 of the interview:

- Simon had been divorced from James's mother for ten years, and had lived with his partner, Angela, for three years.
- At the time of his death, Simon was working as a nursing home manager and Angela was working as a carer. His salary was three times greater than Angela's.
- James is aged 25 and Lucy is aged 23. Neither of them has any children. They are both working and neither of them was dependent on Simon.
- The home in which Simon and Angela lived is worth £200,000 and is owned in Simon's sole name.
- The other assets in Simon's estate amount to approximately £50,000.
- James is concerned about any entitlement that Angela may be able to claim. James would be prepared to be act in any way that is necessary to ensure that the estate can be dealt with, including litigation.

**Example 2: property**

During your ten-minute preparation time after receiving the assessment memorandum, you realised immediately that you needed to discover why Yusuf believed he was entitled to the land. This would inform the direction that you took in stage 2, gathering the information.

In order to continue using this worked example, let's say that you obtained the following facts during the information-gathering in stage 2 of the interview:

- Yusuf has been using land at the bottom part of his garden that is adjacent to his neighbour's back garden. It is a rectangle of approximately 1.5 metres deep by 9 metres wide. See page 28 for Yusuf's hand-drawn plan.
- Yusuf has cultivated this land as a vegetable patch to grow potatoes and onions for the past 15 years. Between the properties is a fence, and his neighbour has threatened to extend that fence to enclose the disputed land as part of her garden.
- The only interaction with the neighbour over this part of the land in the past has been when their children have accidently hit the ball over the fence between the properties and it has landed on the vegetable patch. They always ask for Yusuf to return it and he does so.
- Yusuf needs this area of land to be confirmed as his because he is in the process of selling his house, and prospective buyers have commented on the appeal of this extra land. He is close to negotiating a sale of the property for £200,000 and his priority is to sell quickly.

In both of these examples, you can identify the legal issues of these matters and also what the clients want to achieve. These findings will provide the bedrock of your advice to the clients in stage 3. In order to utilise this information and your understanding, there are two stages. The first is to analyse the information, which is an internal process and will be dealt with very briefly, and the second is to inform the client of the situation.

## ANALYSE THE CLIENT'S LEGAL MATTER

One of the greatest challenges of the SQE2 client interview assessment is that there is no respite between the information-gathering stage, where you gain an understanding of the information that you can use to advise the client, and the part where you need to start communicating your advice. The only time that you have to think about and analyse the situation is when you are summarising the situation back to the client. There are some important points that may assist your approach to analysing the matter:

- Try to keep your analysis of the matter and the repercussions on your advice in your mind throughout the interview. As you move through the information-gathering process, the legal position should begin to crystalise so that you have established the basis of your advice before you begin the summary. In **Example 2: property**, once Yusuf tells you that he has used the land for 15 years, you will be able to internally tick off the time requirement in adverse possession.
- Keep a clear divide in your mind between the legal position and the other options that are open to the client. We recommend that you deal with the legal position first, that is, specifying what the law is, before moving on to non-legal options (we will explore this further in the next section). Keeping these distinct will help you to focus your analysis.
- Do not be afraid to ask the client for a few moments to gather your thoughts. This will allow you to finalise the relevant points in your mind and identify the order in which you want to put them across. This will also make it more likely that the advice will emerge in a clear and concise manner.

---

### Example 2: property

Your advice to Yusuf may be that he has a potential claim but that the neighbour may have the ability to challenge that claim and prevent him from succeeding. This is the legal position.

You will then need to present other non-litigious options to Yusuf, advising what he is able to do at this point, such as consider negotiation, do nothing or proceed with selling the land.

---

## HOW TO PROVIDE THE ADVICE

### Interview technique

Remember that you are advising a client on their specific problem. The client is interested in how you can solve their particular issue, not in a potted history of the law of wills and estates or adverse possession. Bear in mind **AC 2**, which requires you to communicate and explain your advice in a way that is suitable for the client to understand: giving too much legal background to the situation would not demonstrate your competency in providing information to the client in a suitable manner.

### Competency to advise and act

When advising the client, you must have regard to Principle 7 of the SRA Code of Conduct 2019, which states that you must act in the best interests of the client. This has two key implications for your conduct in the interview.

#### Forming balanced advice

You must set out the strengths and weaknesses of the matter to the client, so that they can decide whether or not they wish to proceed with instructing you to act in the matter. Sometimes you might need to give them unwelcome advice, for example that they have no case and will be unlikely to prevail in litigation.

Crucially, your role is to *advise* the client, and the final decision is theirs to make. It is essential to consider this in your SQE2 assessment as there can be a danger of trying to appear too confident and dictating to the client what they should do. This removes their autonomy of choice and would be considered poor interviewing technique. To prove your competency under **AC 5**, you need to manage the client's expectations and inspire their confidence in your ability to act in the matter: these two points should underpin your approach to forming advice.

#### Areas of the law

Principle 7 also means that you must only advise on areas that you are competent to advise on. As you know, your SQE2 client interview assessments will be in the areas of wills/probate and property, on matters that you should already know and understand from the FLK you gained during SQE1. It is very likely that you will be competent to provide preliminary advice.

However, during the questioning in stage 2 of the interview, related matters could arise that you cannot answer immediately or are not competent to deal with. In this situation, you would need to tell the client/assessor that you will perform further research or refer the matter to a colleague at your firm and will provide advice in a future meeting or communication with the client.

## Interview technique

It is expected that at an initial interview the advice will be preliminary, and that you will follow up with a written letter and possibly future meetings. This is underlined by the SRA Assessment Guidance, which states that:

> Candidates do not need to provide detailed advice at this stage. They can conduct the interview on the basis that they will be advising the client in detail at a later date. However, candidates do need to give enough preliminary advice and to address enough of the client's concerns to establish the client's trust and confidence.

Your advice should allow the client to understand, as much as possible, what their situation is, including whether further meetings will be required.

Always avoid giving advice in a casual, 'off-the-cuff' manner, for example saying that the 'Land Registration Act probably applies here'. This is far too casual and imprecise, and will lead to confusion and uncertainty. All legal advice should be properly considered and researched, and giving incorrect advice at any stage of the matter will cause the client to doubt the further advice that you give them. This will break the trust and rapport that you are trying to build with them (competencies under **AC 3** and **AC 5** for the SQE2 assessment). A better way of framing this if advising Yusuf in **Example 2** would be:

> You have a potential claim under what is known as adverse possession. This means that, even though you do not legally own this piece of land, there are some situations where you are entitled to claim it. These are set out in the Land Registration Act and I will now take you through the relevant points.

Remember, however, that the accuracy of your advice will not be assessed for the SQE2 client interview component.

## Communicate with clarity

You need to explain the client's legal position to them in clear language that is easy for them to follow. Communication is a crucial part of the SQE2 client interview assessment and you will need to prove your competencies under **AC 2**:

> Communicate and explain in a way that is suitable for the client to understand.

You need to develop a method for communicating legal principles to a person who does not have a legal background. Here are some tips to follow:

### Avoid using complicated legal terminology and Latin phrases

- Do not use complicated legal terminology or jargon in the client interview. You might be tempted to show off the huge amount of knowledge that you have acquired during your education. The client, however, is not interested in that and simply wants to know what you are talking about; an assessor would regard using jargon as failing to show competency under **AC 2**. Ensure that the client would be able to understand what you are saying without needing to look up words in a dictionary.

  For example, you might use this terminology when discussing adverse possession with legal colleagues:

> To demonstrate a prima facie case of adverse possession under the authority of *Powell v McFarlane* it is incumbent upon the claimant, who would be you, to demonstrate actual possession, *animus possendi*, and that you have satisfied the maxim of *nec vi, nec clam, nec precario …*

However, this would be confusing and unclear to your client, and you would not demonstrate competence under **AC 2** in the assessment. You could use simpler and more direct speech instead:

> To show adverse possession, you need to prove that you have been in actual control of the land and that you intended to exclude others from it. You must show that you have done this without force, openly and without permission.

- If you have to use legal terms such as 'restrictive covenant', 'legal easement', 'age contingency' and 'nil rate band', make sure that you explain what these mean.
- As shown in the example above, do not use antiquated language. The area of wills and probate has historically used many Latin phrases, but clients might not be familiar with them and find this confusing. This table include some examples of Latin phrases to avoid, but it is by no means an exhaustive list.

| Latin phrases | Alternative phrasing |
|---|---|
| Intestate | Dying without a will |
| Commorientes | Two people died at the same time |
| Compos mentis | Of sound mind |
| Locus standi | The right to bring a claim |
| Animus possendi | Intention to possess |

### Check that the client has understood you
Ensure that you check with the client that they have understood the advice that you have given them. This can be done by simply asking the client:

> Do you understand the legal points that I have outlined? Do you have questions about what I have said?

There are two principal reasons for doing this:

- It will help to build the professional rapport between you and the client, a competency requirement under **AC 3**. The client is out of their comfort zone and might need extra support to understand the full implications of your advice.
- In practice, it helps avoid any confusion when you later send out a letter of advice to them and it transpires that they misunderstood something that you have told them in the interview.

### Avoid information overload
Try to stop yourself from overwhelming the client with too much information. Think about what they need to know and what they do not. The client only wants to know how the law applies to their situation.

Provide concise advice, tailored to the client's needs (demonstrating your competency under **AC 4**). For example, do not advise a course of action that is at odds with the client's aims and objectives, or is not feasible in the circumstances for reasons of time or cost.

A red flag that should warn that you are saying too much is when you start talking about hypothetical situations – 'If [x] had happened, then ...'. This can occasionally be helpful to explain a point but more often it is an example of going into too much detail on an irrelevant point.

---

### Example 1: wills and probate

You need to explain to the client the impact of there not being a will.

- Use the phrase 'dying without a will' instead of '*intestate*'.
- You do not need to explore the history of why the provisions of intestacy exist – this is unnecessary and tangential. For example, you could say:

> When someone passes away without leaving a will, there are rules that set out how their estate is to be distributed. The relevant rules that apply here are ...

---

### Example 2: property

You need to explain the meaning of adverse possession to the client. Do not use the words '*animum possendi*' – you can easily substitute this with 'intention to possess' or 'intention to exclude others'. For example:

> You need to show that you have had an intention to exclude others from the land, including the actual owner. You have explained that there is a fence between your land and theirs, and if a neighbour's ball has ever been hit over the fence, you have returned it. This is likely to mean that the test has been met.

There are many fascinating cases that explore the question of whether factual possession has been demonstrated. You do not need to go through these cases; you can simply give examples of how this test can be met, as in the example above.

---

### Reading the client's reaction and responding to their needs

Returning to the theme of multitasking in the client interview assessment, it is important to gauge the reaction of the client at all stages; doing so will demonstrate a client-focused approach as required by **AC 4** and prove your competency in responding to the client's concerns with interest and empathy.

Does the client appear confused, uncertain or upset? If any of these emotions are present, then you need to think about how to react.

- If the client appears confused or uncertain, you might simply need to ask them to confirm that they understand, or whether they have any questions. This is good practice even when the client is not showing visible signs of confusion.
- If the client is upset – and remember that in a wills and probate interview assessment it is likely that the client will have been recently bereaved – you should demonstrate the utmost sensitivity and tact in your interview style. In practice, you might offer a short break in the interview if the client is too upset to continue, but, as you know, the SQE2 client interview assessment is timed, so offering a break is not to be recommended. You could, however, offer the client a moment to compose themselves before restarting the interview.

---

### Example 1: wills and probate

If the client appears to be distressed or is struggling to find the right words, this example is a tactful way of proceeding:

James Smith:     My dad works ... I mean, he worked ... I ... [*client struggling to phrase tenses because of his father's recent passing*].

Candidate:        It's fine, I understand that these can be difficult matters to talk about. Please do take your time. I am here to listen and help you through this.

This can be difficult because you will be very aware of the time in this assessment, and you might be tempted to correct the client with the correct tense and then move on. Try to resist this, because a central part of the interviewing process is helping the client to work through the information themselves so that they can give you the facts, without you needing to interpret half-facts.

---

### Assessment technique

The assessor who is role-playing the client is, of course, not actually bereaved, but they may act in a particular way if the client brief instructs them to do so. Reaffirming the concern at this stage that you might have expressed at the start of a wills and probate interview is a good way of demonstrating your client-centred approach (and proving your competency under **AC 4**).

---

## THE ADVICE

Candidates can find it challenging to know where to start when providing advice, particularly when required to advise first on a broad issue and then on smaller, specific points. As a general rule, it is useful to provide the legal advice first and then move on to the non-legal (practical) advice. This is because the legal advice explains the situation to the client whilst the non-legal advice focuses on their options. The client needs to understand the former, but the latter will generally be far more important for them.

There are exceptions to this:

- There might be different items within a will to consider, such as multiple specific bequests, and you could decide that it is easier to deal with the legal position and non-legal choices for each one in turn.
- The client might intervene to ask a specific non-legal question whilst you are explaining the legal position. We would recommend answering the client's question, as this demonstrates your flexibility and client-centred approach (**AC 4**). Remember that it is the client's interview, and your responsibility is to ensure that the process is tailored to them.

### Legal advice

Providing legal advice means explaining to the client their position with respect of the law. This comprises two components:

1.    Briefly explain the law and apply the facts of the case to it.
2.    Give specific advice.

*Brief explanation and application of facts*

Keep your explanation of the law brief, clear and easy to understand at all times: in the SQE2 client interview assessment, this is crucial for demonstrating your competencies under **AC 2**:

> Communicate and explain in a way that is suitable for the client to understand.

Follow these points to meet this assessment criterion:

- Do not go into too much depth on the relevant legislation and only focus on the parts that affect your client's case.
- Remember to explain legal terms when you have to use technical language.
- Make sure your client understands that the answer to their issue might not be straightforward and could depend on a number of factors.

## Example 1: wills and probate

You might begin your advice in the following way:

> I understand that your father, Simon, passed away without leaving a will. In such circumstances, assets owned by the deceased will usually pass to the next of kin – I'll talk about that more in a minute – and two people need to be appointed to deal with his estate.

This example identifies the first crucial legal point and explains what it means, without unnecessarily using legal terminology such as intestacy. Later in the interview you would need to explain the role of an executor and the responsibility that it would entail, but the central legal principle has been clearly communicated here.

## Example 2: property

You might begin your advice in the following way:

> One of the ways that you can be entitled to land that is not legally yours is through something called 'adverse possession'. This means that if you use the land for a period of time and meet certain requirements you become entitled to the land and the current owner has no right to it. There are different tests depending on whether the land is registered or unregistered. You have told me that it is registered. The requirements are …

This example identifies the legal point of adverse possession and explains what it means. The first part of providing legal advice is therefore achieved.

*Specific legal advice*

Using clear language and avoiding or explaining legal terms, you will need to explain the more precise points of law and their impact on the client's situation. This is an opportunity for you to demonstrate your ability to provide client-focused advice, as required under **AC 4**.

Make sure that the amount of information you provide at every stage is manageable for the client, and check their understanding at different stages of your explanation.

## Interview technique

You can reassure the client by acknowledging that you have provided them with a lot of complex information and want to check that they have understood it so far.

You could ask a few questions at this point that might not have been relevant earlier but, as a general rule, do not reopen the information-gathering stage as that can confuse the structure of the interview.

Crucially, you need to ensure that by the end of the interview the client understands what their legal position is, including any strengths or weaknesses of their case and any requirements they will need to satisfy to make a claim. The type of legal advice you need to give will vary for each interview and each area of law.

## Example 1: wills and probate

Your specific advice could be as follows:

> The main subject that we will be talking about is Simon's estate. This means what he left for others to divide between them. As I said, two administrators are necessary to deal with the estate, and we will talk about that shortly.

> The crucial question in any estate, and I apologise if this seems blunt, is what the assets are, and where they go.

> The key question is to find out who is Simon's 'next of kin', which means his closest living relative. If a person is married, their next of kin is usually their husband or wife, and they would normally inherit automatically. As Angela was not married to Simon, this is not the case for her.

> That means that the estate will pass to his children equally – to you and your sister Lucy. You have told me that you are both over 18, and because you are not minors you can inherit from the estate. This is the starting point, and you will therefore each receive half of the estate.

> Is there anything so far that you would like me to explain further?

> The next question is what is included in the estate. You have confirmed that Simon owned his property by himself, so this will be part of the estate. All other assets owned by him, including money, shares etc, will also be part of the estate. It looks as though the value of the estate is approximately £250,000 [*this is based on the figures that James told you about in the questioning*]. If Simon had any debts, they will be paid from the estate, so the total value might be less than this amount.

> The next question is whether anyone has any claim against the property. You have told me that Simon had no other living relatives, and so the only person who might seek to claim is Angela.

> In situations like this, the law allows certain people to make a claim that they have not been reasonably provided for by a will. Because of Angela's relationship to Simon and the fact she lived with him for more than three years, she is eligible to make a claim. If she does this, the court would determine whether reasonable provision has been made for her or whether some money from Simon's estate should be paid to her. The court would look at the whole situation to determine what would be reasonable in all of the circumstances. She has six months from the date that probate was granted to make this claim.

It is important to deliver the perhaps unwelcome news to the client that they cannot stop the claim, and that Angela might have a strong case because of the length of her relationship with Simon. You would need to prepare James and his sister Lucy for an outcome where their portion of the remaining estate after other debts are paid might be further reduced. Your competency under **AC 3** would be assessed here: you are required to treat the client with respect and courtesy, and to be sensitive when preparing the client for a potentially difficult or unwelcome outcome.

There will of course be follow-up questions to these points, and the sample interviews provided in Chapters 7 and 8 show how you might deal with such questions.

You would also need to finish your legal advice to the client by calculating whether inheritance tax would be payable, although remember to make it clear that this would be subject to a precise calculation after all assets and liabilities of the estate have been collected. It is unlikely that clients will have enough information to give a definitive answer at an initial client interview, but you can often give a clear indication as inheritance tax does not start to be paid until the value of the estate exceeds £325,000.

## Assessment technique

When gathering information in the wills and probate interview, it is normally a good idea to get some background information about anyone whose name is mentioned in the will, including whether they are alive, their relationship to the deceased, and whether or not they have been in contact. A number of potential issues will often be discovered just with some simple questions about named people.

## Example 2: property

Your specific advice could be as follows:

> The key question is whether or not you have the right to this strip of land. You need to satisfy four requirements:

> The first is time – the properties are registered so you need to have been using the land for at least ten years. You told me that you began using the land 15 years ago, so that is fine.

Secondly, you need to have shown control over the land. 'Showing control' can mean many things and depends on the facts. You have told me that you have grown crops there continuously and that you tend to them daily between 3 PM and 4 PM. Every year you harvest the vegetables and replant seeds. I cannot say it is certain, but it is likely that you have shown control, so the second test is probably satisfied.

So far, do you understand?

Thirdly, you need to demonstrate that you treated the land as your own and did not merely borrow it. Using the land to plant vegetables may satisfy this requirement.

Finally, you must have done all of this without the neighbour consenting to you using their land – this would demonstrate that they control the land. You must not have used force and you must have used it openly without secrecy, so that the neighbour can see that it is being used. Again, it appears that you have satisfied this requirement.

Based on the information you have provided today, you have likely met the criteria for adverse possession. However, that is not the end of the matter. Even though you have met these criteria, your neighbour can challenge your rights if they wish. I will go into detail about how you can try to have the land transferred to you in a moment, but the crucial point is that you would need to ask the Land Registry to approve the transfer. They will ask the neighbour for their views and it is likely, from what you have said, that they will object. If they do object, you would have to establish one of two points in order to succeed:

First, you must show that the original plans are unclear, and that you used the land in the mistaken but reasonable belief that you were entitled to it. I will need to look at your property's plans to see how clear they are, but this may be a possibility for you.

Second, if the plans are clear, you would have to show that it would be unconscionable for the neighbour to retain this land. This is a very hard test to meet, and would require you to show that it would be completely unfair and unreasonable for them to gain the land back. We would have to investigate this issue further, but the important points for you to note are (1) it would take time because the neighbour is entitled to 13 weeks' notice, and (2) you may or may not succeed in a claim.

> I appreciate that this may not be what you wanted to hear, and that it is a lot of information to take in. I will provide further advice about the options available to you in a moment, but first I'd like to check that you understand your position based on this information.

This example set out the tests very simply and then applies each point to the client's case. This particular example is quite straightforward but now would be the time to discuss any weaknesses that the client has in respect of these requirements, so that they are aware of both the strengths and weaknesses of their case.

## Assessment technique

When dealing with property, always check how the property is held. If it is owned by more than one person, the immediate follow-up questions should be the identity of the other person(s), and whether the client knows how the property was held, that is, as joint tenants or tenants in common. You will know from your SQE1 FLK that this makes a considerable difference. In **Example 2** the property is owned by the client alone and so this does not apply, but if the property is jointly owned it is an essential question to ask. See **Revise SQE: Property Law and Practice** to revise this topic.

### Non-legal advice and setting out the client's options

You might think that providing legal advice is the most important part of the advice in an interview. In fact, it only tells the client about their legal position and does not help them to understand how, if at all, their problem could be resolved or their goals achieved. This is why the second part of the advice is so important: what options are available?

In the first part of the interview you will have discovered the client's objectives in coming to see you. Having given some preliminary legal advice on the client's matter, you should return to these objectives and set out the client's options in proceeding with the matter. You need to adopt a client-centred approach, as required by **AC 4**.

## Interview technique

To demonstrate your competency under **AC 4**, you need to show that you can understand the client's problem from their own perspective, not just the legal position.

Your role is therefore not to tell the client what they should do (or indeed what you would do) but rather enable them to understand their legal position and the options available to them so that they can, in turn, make an informed decision about what to do.

1. The legal options. This will almost always be court action (it is feasible that a lease may have a clause that requires the parties to use arbitration in the event of a dispute, but this is not likely to occur). The strength of the case that you have identified will influence the effectiveness of this option, but there are other points to consider, including the likely time, cost, and potential damage to relationships.

2.  The non-legal options. These will probably form a large part of your advice as they include the other steps that the client can take, such as negotiation, trying to resolve the matter informally and taking more practical steps. For example, in **Example 1: wills and probate**, a non-legal option might be to reach out to the partner of the deceased to try to ascertain her position.

The non-legal, practical advice might fall into two categories:

1.  How should the client follow up on what you have advised in respect of the law?
2.  Are there any other options?

You can address these questions in any order, although the first point tends to follow more logically from providing the legal advice, so we recommend dealing with this first. Therefore, if you have advised the client that they have a strong legal case, it might be appropriate to deal with how this might work first, and explain the process for issuing a claim and the potential time and costs consequences. You can then move on to alternative options.

## Example 2: property

Following on from page 48, your legal advice to the client is that they have a possible claim to the land but that there are challenges.

Your first piece of practical advice would be how to assert that claim if Yusuf wanted to – by writing to the Land Registry with a completed notice asking for the land to be transferred to his title. You would then explain what the process would be (complete the appropriate form; provide evidence of occupation; enclose the relevant fee and send it to the Land Registry), what might happen next, and the advantages and disadvantages.

Advantages:

- This is the only way to formalise ownership without the consent of the neighbour.
- The neighbour will have to respond.

Disadvantages:

- The process will be long (probably at least 6 to 12 months).
- There would be costs involved.
- The claim is far from strong.

This is a good example of why it is essential to understand the client's goals and objectives. Yusuf clearly wants the land, because of the imminent sale of his own house. When explaining the advantages and disadvantages to him, you would need to emphasise the following:

- A pending application to the Land Registry will take time. The sale might be delayed if the buyer wants to wait until it is completed.
- If the neighbour objects to the application to register the land in Yusuf's name, which they are entitled to do, it might cause friction between the client and the neighbour. This would have to be disclosed to any purchaser, which could delay the sale.

This option might lead to the client's own primary concerns not being satisfied.

It is therefore vital to look at alternative options that might help the client to achieve their goals. Remember that your advice should be driven by Principle 7 of the SRA

Code of Conduct 2019 – to act in your client's best interests. To abide by this principle and prove your competency under **AC 4** and **AC 5**, tailor the options to the client's case, and do not simply provide a shopping list of different possibilities that might be completely inappropriate to this situation.

Other options you might suggest to the client in this scenario:

- Do not introduce a delay to the sale by applying to register the title. Consider in more detail the value difference between including the land in the sale or not.
- Negotiate with the neighbour. Suggest that either the client or you (acting on behalf of the client) try to negotiate a compromise on the ownership of the land. (See Chapter 5 for more information and guidance on developing your negotiation skills.)

The options can be varied and creative as long as they are clearly relevant to the case. Remember to think practically here and set out the advantages and disadvantages of each option to enable the client to make an informed decision.

## NEXT STEPS

When you and the client have discussed the legal options and they have decided which option best meets their objectives, you will then need to agree the next steps to take in the matter:

- Agree a plan of action and the extent of your instructions with the client.
- Clearly explain the steps that you intend to take in this matter.
- Provide a potential timescale for achieving the client's objectives.

This last point is important: a frequent complaint made by clients about their legal advisers is not being kept fully informed about timescales or knowing when they should expect to be contacted. Being clear about the timeframe and likely future contact is conducive to maintaining an effective professional relationship with the client, as stipulated under **AC 5**.

### Example 1: wills and probate

In this scenario you could discuss the following next steps with James (the client):

- As his father Simon died intestate, a grant of letters of administration would need to be applied for before his estate can be distributed.
- One administrator is required to apply for the grant, although it is desirable to have two in order to share the responsibility. You could suggest that James and/or his sister Lucy could act as administrators of Simon's estate.
- Explain to James that no distribution of the estate should be made until at least six months after the grant of letters of administration, because a claim might be brought by Simon's partner, Angela. This is under the Inheritance (Provision for Family and Dependants) Act 1975, although remember that you would not need to tell the client the specific law.
- Because Angela has six months after the grant of the letters of administration to bring a claim, there will be no certainty as to whether Angela will make a claim until after this point.
- If the administrators distribute Simon's estate less than six months after the grant, and Angela does make a claim, the administrators would be personally liable to pay any amount that she is entitled to.
- Any liability to pay inheritance tax must be established and paid before Simon's estate is distributed.

The legal advice is not such that it would lead to an active response by the client; unlike the property scenario in **Example 2**, there is no question of making a claim themselves. The legal follow-up to this would be to apply for letters of administration, wait to see whether Angela plans to do anything and then react accordingly.

There are, however, some additional points that might be considered, including reaching out to Angela to discuss the matter with her. This might help James to understand her position and whether she has sought or is planning to seek legal advice. This advice exemplifies the importance of asking questions about family history early in the interview, because in this instance it would help you to understand whether or not James and Angela are on speaking terms. If not, this suggestion should be made with greater caution.

These points should be discussed with James at this initial client interview and followed up in a letter of advice.

## ■ STAGE 4: CONCLUDE THE INTERVIEW

There are some key points that you should cover before formally closing the interview:

1.  Recap and summarise:
    *   the legal advice, non-legal advice and practical options you have provided
    *   the client's decision on how to proceed in the matter or, if they have not decided yet, confirmation that this is the situation.

    Check with the client that they have fully understood their options, your advice and the proposed next steps. Ask whether they would like you to clarify any aspects of the case.
2.  If you need any further information or documentation from the client, remind them to bring it to the office on another occasion or send it to you. In a wills and probate claim, further information or documentation could include:
    *   copy of the death certificate
    *   title deeds to any property
    *   bank account details
    *   stocks and shares certificates
    *   evidence of any valuations of the estate's assets.

    For James's case in **Example 1**, you might ask for any evidence of valuation of the property, and the death certificate.
3.  Make sure that the client is aware of how long the matter is expected to take. As discussed in the previous section, this is an important aspect of managing the client's expectations, required by **AC 5**. You do not have to be specific as there is often no certainty around this, but you do need to give relevant dates. For **Example 1**, you would need to remind James that Angela has six months to bring a claim for a share of the estate.
4.  Check that you both agree on who will make the next contact – either you or the client.
5.  If the client requires any further information about their matter, remind them of who to contact and provide contact details. Whilst this will normally be you, it is a good idea to say that there are others in the firm who can be contacted if you are not available, and that contact details will be provided in the client care letter to follow.
6.  Ask the client whether there is anything else you can help them with, before telling them that the interview is now formally concluded. You might conclude the interview in the following way:

Thank you for coming in today to see me. I understand that this has been a difficult discussion and I hope that I have provided some clarity. The letter will be with you within 14 days and, if you have any questions arising from it, please do contact me. Is there anything else I can help you with before we conclude?

## TIME MANAGEMENT

During the interview you should be aware of the passing of time, because you want to conclude the interview shortly before time expires. Aim to provide all advice to the client by 24 minutes, so that you have a minute spare to end the interview.

| Assessment technique |
| --- |
| Note down the time that the interview starts and ends, using the same timepiece to avoid inconsistencies. This will enable you to:<br><br>• ensure that you have been allowed the full amount of time in the interview<br>• know at any point how long you have left<br>• log on the attendance note how long the interview took. |

## ■ SUMMARY AND REFLECTION

We hope that this chapter has provided useful suggestions to help you approach stages 3 and 4 of the interview assessment, providing advice and concluding the interview. As with stages 1 and 2, there are many chances to demonstrate your competency under the SQE2 assessment criteria, such as:

• **AC 2**: communicate your advice to the client in a clear and precise way, using language that they will understand.
• **AC 3**: be polite and sensitive to the client when delivering unwelcome news.
• **AC 4**: understand the issue from the client's perspective and provide advice that will deliver their objective.
• **AC 5**: manage the client's expectations by explaining the limitations of some options, so that they can make an informed decision and feel confident in your ability to take the case forward.

This chapter and Chapter 2 have provided some guidance on how to prepare yourself for each stage of the interview assessment so that you can remain calm, professional and in control. All stages of the SQE2 client interview assessment bring their own particular pitfalls:

• You might be especially nervous at the start of the interview, stage 1.
• During stage 2, information-gathering, you might be concerned about the interview stalling.
• The big risk with stage 3, giving advice, is losing track of time as you discuss different options and lay out the next steps.
• Lack of time might cause you to rush the conclusion to the interview, stage 4, and end your conversation with the client abruptly.

Take some time to consider how you can adapt our suggested structure to your own interview style, to maximise your chances of proving your competence in all elements of the SQE2 client interviewing assessment criteria.

# 4

# The attendance note and legal analysis

You will be relieved when the client interview has concluded, but the SQE2 client interview assessment is not over at this point: you have a further 25 minutes to write an attendance note and legal analysis of the interview that has been conducted. This is the same amount of time as is allocated for the interview, which emphasises the importance of this part of the assessment.

The attendance note represents a detailed summary of the action that you have taken in connection to a client's case. The purpose of an attendance note is to provide:

• a contemporaneous record of the case
• a guide for others on the status of the case, including your analysis of the case to ensure consistency with any follow-up action taken by others
• a to-do list.

We recommend that you bear these points in mind as you approach this part of the assessment, as they will help to shape your response.

This chapter will give a detailed commentary on each aspect of the discrete assessment criteria for this element of the SQE2 assessment. Guidance on best practice and how to prepare for writing the attendance note is then provided, followed by our suggestions on how to structure an attendance note so that you can meet the requirements of the SQE2 assessment criteria and prove your competence in this component.

Detailed guidance and information about legal writing for the SQE2 assessments is provided in ***Introduction to Written Legal Skills for SQE2***. You will be able to transfer the skills you have developed when revising for the written skills assessments to this part of the client interview assessment.

## ■ ATTENDANCE NOTE/LEGAL ANALYSIS ASSESSMENT CRITERIA AND COMMENTARY

It is important to remember that the assessment criteria for the attendance note/legal analysis are different from the criteria for the client interview. The broad assessment criteria for the interview focus on the relationship between the candidate and the client, whilst the assessment criteria for the attendance note/legal analysis focus on the candidate's accuracy in setting out the information related to the interview they have conducted and their analysis of the client's legal position. This is a crucial difference: during the interview you won't be assessed on your knowledge of the law, but your understanding of the law in respect of the interview *will* be tested in the attendance note. This is underpinned by the SRA's objective of the assessment, for candidates to:

demonstrate they are able to produce an attendance note recording a client interview and initial legal analysis.

> ## SQE2 attendance note/legal analysis assessment criteria
>
> Try to remember these points as you construct your attendance note:
>
> ### Skills
> 1. Record all relevant information.
> 2. Identify appropriate next steps.
> 3. Provide client-focused advice (ie advice that demonstrates an understanding of the problem from the client's point of view and what the client wants to achieve, not just from a legal perspective).
>
> ### Application of law
> 4. Apply the law correctly to the client's situation.
> 5. Apply the law comprehensively to the client's situation, identifying any ethical and professional conduct issues and exercising judgement to resolve them honestly and with integrity.

See the Appendix for a full record of the SRA's performance indicators in respect of these criteria. A summary of their points of competency is given alongside the assessment criteria commentary below.

Let's explore each assessment criterion in more detail.

## SKILLS ASSESSMENT CRITERIA

### 1. Record all relevant information

It is important to make a note of what happened in the interview as soon as is practically possible after the meeting. As time passes, your recollections will inevitably vary as to what was said, and these inconsistencies will only increase. In practice, and depending on the firm, an attendance note might also be sent out to the client, for them to confirm that this was what was said and offer any thoughts on the content.

Even in a small firm, you will not be the only person with conduct of the case file. Although you might be largely responsible for it, there will be times when other people need to review the file and determine what has happened at any point. This could be a partner, an associate, a trainee, an auditor or, in the event of the file being transferred to a different firm, an entirely new solicitor. The note therefore needs to be capable of conveying to a reader who was not present at the meeting a record of what happened, so that they can link the information to the rest of the file.

Therefore, the attendance note seeks to ensure that the content of what was discussed in the meeting is clear and can be understood by everyone: the interviewer, the client and anyone new to the case. Whilst it is not meant to be a verbatim statement of the meeting, it should contain sufficient detail and depth to reflect what happened.

You will demonstrate **competence** if you can:

- identify the key facts from the assessment materials and your conversation with the client in the interview
- include only facts that are important for achieving the client's objectives and are relevant to the legal analysis.

You will **not** demonstrate **competence** if your attendance note:

• does not include the relevant facts from the assessment materials or the client interview
• includes facts that are irrelevant or unrelated to your legal advice.

This assessment criterion underlines the importance of adopting a methodical approach to your client interview as discussed in Chapters 2 and 3, because this will make it much easier to write the attendance note. At each stage of the interview you will have identified the important information and noted it down, so that at this stage, you can quickly feed it into the attendance note.

The summary of facts that we discussed at the end of Chapter 2 will also be useful here: when you summarised the facts to the client, that was your opportunity to check that the facts that you later include in the attendance note are accurate.

---

### Attendance note/legal analysis technique

When approaching this part of the assessment, remember that you will be writing with a full understanding of the case. Try to put yourself in the mindset of someone reading the note without that understanding, and make sure that you include the key points of information on which you have based your advice. Do not worry about stating the obvious – small details might be central to a new reader trying to understand the case.

---

## 2. Identify appropriate next steps

The attendance note must clearly identify your recommendations for the next steps in the case. This could be as broad as providing the client with a follow-up letter containing a summary of the meeting and reviewing the options that have been suggested, or as specific as issuing legal proceedings once the necessary funds have been received from the client. In all cases, you need to provide a checklist of the next tasks to be undertaken, which can be referred to and easily understood by anyone else dealing with the case.

You will demonstrate **competence** if you set out the next steps necessary to progress the client's matter, such as sending a letter of advice to the client or requesting further information from them.

You will **not** demonstrate **competence** if:

• you do not include the next steps to take in the case
• the steps you suggest do not help to progress the case and are irrelevant to the client's issue.

We recommend that you do this twice, first in detail whilst you identify the points of discussion in the attendance note, and then briefly at the end so that there is a clear list of tasks to be completed. This would allow anyone reading the file to go straight to the end and see what progress has been made, checking off the relevant points when needed.

---

### Example 1: wills and probate

The next steps for this case might be:

1.   James to provide valuation of the property.
2.   James to obtain letters of administration and provide evidence to the firm of completion.
3.   James to notify the firm in the event of any contact from Angela.
4.   Diarise six months from letters being granted as the deadline for Angela to apply to the court to make a claim under the Inheritance (Provision for Family and Dependants) Act 1975.

## 3. Provide client-focused advice (ie advice that demonstrates an understanding of the problem from the client's point of view and what the client wants to achieve, not just from a legal perspective)

The requirements for this criterion are very similar to **AC 4** for the client interview and reiterate a point that has made throughout this book: you need to tailor your approach to the client's specific situation, and understand what they want to gain from the legal process. These principles should inform your advice when writing your attendance note. Do not include a potted history of the legal issues but focus on acting in the client's best interests (Principle 7 of the SRA Code of Conduct 2019).

You will demonstrate **competence** if you:

- demonstrate an understanding of the client's problem from their perspective
- address any relevant commercial considerations and/or the client's personal circumstances, priorities, objectives and constraints.

You will **not** demonstrate **competence** if you:

- do not approach or appreciate the client's problem from the client's perspective
- do not focus on the issues identified by the client.

Remember that you need to set out legal and non-legal (practical) advice, based on what the *client* wants to achieve rather than what *you* might prefer to do. Insisting on litigation when the client wants to avoid hostility with the other party will not demonstrate client-focus, and you should be led by your client's goals when writing your advice in the attendance note.

### Example 2: property

You might state that Yusuf's primary concern was to try to sell the property as quickly as possible. For this reason, you suggested in the interview that he might want to negotiate an agreement with the neighbour or simply proceed with the sale regardless, as both of these options would be faster than applying for the land to be transferred to his title and risking the neighbour's opposition.

## APPLICATION OF LAW ASSESSMENT CRITERIA

### 4. Apply the law correctly to the client's situation

When writing your attendance note, it is essential for you to demonstrate several skills in respect of the application of law: identify the relevant principles, state the law correctly, and apply the law to the client's case.

*Identify the relevant principles and state the law correctly*
To identify legal principles, start with a broad approach and progressively narrow it down. The narrower your focus becomes, the more precise you can be, but you also risk giving advice that is less accurate. The starting point of identifying the broad legal principles should not be difficult and you should be able to clearly state the law relating to your client's case.

### Example 2: property

Yusuf was seeking your advice in respect of an adverse possession issue with his neighbour. In the attendance note, you should set out the requirements that flow from that issue and state (if appropriate) that you explained these to Yusuf.

Because the accuracy of your legal knowledge will be assessed in the attendance note, remember to write down any legal points that occur to you at this stage that you did not think about during the interview. If this happens, add this as an action point at the end of your note, as a reminder that you need to make the client aware of this missed point in the follow-up letter.

### Apply the law to the client's case

You should be able to identify legal principles and state the law quite quickly, as these are broad statements. Setting out the application to the client's case will require more time. To achieve this assessment criterion, you should identify the relevant facts in turn and link them to the legal points. End each point by stating how you advised the client on this aspect and (if different) what the correct position is.

This is a crucial part of the attendance note as you will need to recall, through memory or notes, the information that the client gave to you and quickly apply the law to it. In order to make your note as efficient and succinct as possible (remember that you have only 25 minutes to write your attendance note), try to adopt a clear structure: use headings to ensure that the reader can move directly to the points of particular importance to them.

You will demonstrate **competence** if you can identify the relevant fundamental legal principles and apply them correctly.

You will **not** demonstrate **competence** if you:

- cannot identify the relevant legal principles
- do not correctly apply those legal principles to the client's case in a way that addresses their needs and concerns.

## 5. Apply the law comprehensively to the client's situation, identifying any ethical and professional conduct issues and exercising judgement to resolve them honestly and with integrity

Whilst **AC 4** deals with the types of issue to be applied, **AC 5** applies to depth of legal analysis. When exploring the relevant facts, you must draw out enough information to fully engage with the legal analysis, and you will be expected to review the arguments that could be made for and against your client's case in order to provide clear and appropriate preliminary advice.

This criterion specifically mentions the rules of professional conduct and ethics. It is essential, therefore, that if an ethical issue arises you look to address it whilst writing your note, and explain what you should, or in some cases must, do in response. Remember that this is a document that must reflect the case to a new reader, and you should demonstrate your knowledge of ethics and professional conduct to your assessor. See *Revise SQE: Ethics and Professional Conduct* to revise these issues.

Finally, there is an emphasis in the performance indicators on conclusions. It is not enough to simply say what the law is and how it applies to the facts. You also need to give a conclusion, even if it is one that can only set out the likely position.

You will demonstrate **competence** if:

- your legal analysis is 'sufficiently detailed' in the context of the client's case
- you can demonstrate that you are evaluating relevant information to identify key issues and risks, and can reach reasonable conclusions
- you refer to pertinent ethical issues and/or the SRA Principles and rules of professional conduct.

You will **not** demonstrate **competence** if:

- your analysis is not 'sufficiently detailed' – you demonstrate little or no understanding of the key issues and risks, and do not reach reasonable conclusions as you have failed to apply the law to the facts
- you do not refer to pertinent ethical issues and/or the SRA Principles and rules of professional conduct.

## ■ TIPS FOR PREPARING TO WRITE THE ATTENDANCE NOTE

As we have established, the attendance note should include detailed information that is clear and enables anyone reading it to understand the fundamental points of the case progression. You should therefore consider the following central points for the interview itself:

- Take notes during the interview.
- Be clear on details. In particular, write down:
  - advice given rather than anticipated
  - deadlines
  - what happens next
  - time taken on interview.

### TAKE NOTES DURING THE INTERVIEW

As we said in Chapter 2 at page 12, it is essential that you take notes during the interview. This will help you to recall facts during the interview, and your interview notes will be vital after the interview when writing your attendance note. We advise you to refer back to our earlier advice and guidance on note-taking.

| Assessment technique |
| --- |
| When you practise interviewing with colleagues or friends, as suggested in Chapter 1, take the opportunity to practise note-taking as well. |

### BE CLEAR ON DETAILS

It is a matter for you to judge what to write down but remember our advice in Chapter 2 that you are aiming to establish a clear chronology of what happened and the impact of events. In order to do this, you should certainly aim to have a note of any dates, names and contact details that emerge from the interview. These will allow you to provide the necessary level of detail in the attendance note, to ensure that whoever reads the file is able to follow precisely what happened.

You will need to ascertain some key details in the wills and probate interview:

- It is essential to be clear on dates of the matter. Identifying that the deceased died in early June, for example, is less helpful and professional than stating that the deceased died on 3 June. This might be particularly important when considering details for inheritance tax purposes.
- You will need to make a clear note of the assets of the estate that are known to the client, as this will form a valuable part of your attendance note.

For the property interview:

- Relevant information will include the details of the property and contact details for any other party with whom you might need to correspond as part of the case.
- If there is a dispute about ownership, you should note down who has legal interests in the property and who has equitable interests.

If the client says something during the interview that is not clear, or you did not fully understand because they spoke too quickly or you were writing a note on something else, do not be afraid to ask them to repeat themselves. This helps to demonstrate your awareness of the value of what the client is saying (remember **AC 1** of the client interview, the importance of listening carefully to the client) and allows you to fulfil **AC 1** of the attendance note/legal analysis – record all relevant information.

## Advice given rather than anticipated

You might have anticipated the potential areas for which advice would be required, both in advance of the day and whilst reading the SQE2 memorandum during the ten-minute preparation time before the interview. You may also have made notes during that ten-minute preparation period. It is therefore crucial that, as the interview takes place, your notes set out the advice you actually *gave* to the client, as opposed to the advice that you *planned* on giving to the client. The risk is that your memory might play tricks on you, and when you read over your notes after the interview whilst preparing to write the attendance note you might think that you gave advice that you did not.

---

### Interview technique

Here are two methods to ensure that you correctly note the advice given rather than anticipated:

- Divide your writing pad into two columns. In the ten-minute period, write your planned thoughts in the left-hand column. During the course of the interview, write your actual advice in the right-hand column.
- Before the interview, make a list of advice points that might be relevant to the case. During the interview, tick off the points that you use, and write down your additional new advice.

Choose whichever method suits you best (or think of other methods), so that you can be sure that you only insert advice that has been given to the client into the attendance note.

---

## Deadlines

Deadlines can be the most important element of an attendance note, because a solicitor's worst fear is missing a deadline, whether a court-imposed timeframe or, even worse, a limitation deadline. This is a key detail that you must write down correctly during the interview and set out (perhaps underlined and emphasised) in the attendance note.

---

### Example 1: wills and probate

This point is particularly relevant in the wills and probate interview, because any claim under the Inheritance Act to vary the terms of a will must be brought within six months of the grant of probate. This should therefore be clearly communicated to the client and the dates added to your notes, together with the actual date of six months after the grant of probate if that action has already occurred.

Including this kind of detail ensures that anyone reading the attendance note would be immediately drawn to the significance of this date.

## What happens next

As we mentioned in Chapter 3, you must discuss the next steps in the interview for both you and the client, so that all parties are clear on what has been agreed. During the interview you should write down these plans, so that when you come to write the attendance note you can produce a checklist of steps and tasks to be achieved. This would allow someone else working on the file to know immediately what remains to be done in this case, and be able to tick off items that have been completed.

## Time taken on interview

Include the start and end times of the client interview in the attendance note. This shows your organisation and control of the interview (as required by **AC 3** of the client interview assessment criteria). The legal world is still dominated by the billable hour, and being able to note this is helpful for when you subsequently have the file reviewed.

## ■ HOW TO STRUCTURE AN ATTENDANCE NOTE

You can choose your own structure for the attendance note but make sure that your note includes all of the correct elements to meet the assessment criteria. You might find it helpful to follow the suggested structure provided in Table 5.1.

*Table 5.1: A suggested structure for the attendance note*

| Section of attendance note | What to include in this section |
|---|---|
| Heading | Begin the attendance note with a heading that will allow the reader to identify quickly what the document is about. You should include the date, time (in practice, this is useful for billing purposes), the name of the client and the title of the matter. |
| Introduction | It is useful to set out a clear introduction to the attendance note which summarises the situation. Your purpose is to provide a clear and succinct summary for the reader on the basis that they have not read the file. |
| Summary of facts | Summarise the key facts that you drew out from the assessment materials and the information-gathering part of the interview (stage 2, as explored in Chapter 2). Remember that you do not need to include every fact, only those that you believe are relevant to the advice (as required by **AC 1**). For example, your introductory conversations to break the ice (recommended for stage 1 of the interview; see Chapter 2), such as talking about the client's journey to the office, do not need to be included. |
| | However, any facts that relates to the legal issue at hand should be included. Bear in mind the requirements of **AC 4** and **AC 5** for the attendance note/legal analysis – you will need to apply the law correctly and comprehensively to the facts of the client's case. |
| Summary of advice | The next stage is to include a summary of your advice for the client. This must be the advice that you actually gave to the client during the interview, and not advice that in hindsight you should have given! The note must be a true record of the interview, and it is essential that anyone else looking at the file would be able to clearly identify the current situation of the case, not the situation that you might now want it to be. |

*(continued)*

*Table 5.1: (continued)*

| Section of attendance note | What to include in this section |
|---|---|
| | Remember to demonstrate your competency under **AC 3** for the attendance note, by providing client-focused advice tailored to the client's own objective in bringing this matter to you. It makes sense, as suggested in Chapter 3, to set out the legal advice first, then the options that follow from the legal advice, before setting out the more practical options. |
| Next steps – for the client | This part of the note addresses the requirements of **AC 2**, identifying appropriate next steps. Using concise and precise language, set out the actions that you agreed the client would take. |
| | It is often easier for the reader (and in this case your assessor) if you lay these out as bullet points, particularly if there is more than one item to list. In practice, this is also neater if the client's next steps involve providing you with documents such as a death certificate, as you could tick off the item once it has been received. |
| Next steps – for the firm | Finally, set out the steps that you will be taking next. This will normally include sending out a client care letter, but may also involve:<br>• doing additional legal research<br>• clarifying some details<br>• adding additional points to the advice that you missed in the interview. |
| | Again, setting this out as a bullet-point list is clear for your assessor, and in practice would allow you to tick off items once they have been completed. |

Below are sample attendance notes/legal analyses following this structure for the two worked examples set out in the introduction. Bear in mind that for the SQE2 client assessment you will be provided with a more detailed case, and so the attendance note would be longer than the notes for our two examples here.

---

### ATTENDANCE NOTE/LEGAL ANALYSIS
### Example 1: wills and probate

**Date:**    DD/MM/YY
**Time:**    10.00–10.25
**Client:**   James Smith
**Matter:**   Estate of Simon Smith, deceased

Attending James Smith regarding late father's estate – Simon Smith. He died intestate. Client concerned about his and his sister's entitlement to the estate; deceased cohabited with a new partner.

#### Deceased:

**DOB:**         01/01/1960
**DOD:**         26/01/2025
**Occupation:**  Retired
**Will:**         No will

#### Family

Client is one of two children of Simon – he has a sister, Lucy Smith. Client is 25 and his sister is 23.

No other living relatives but Simon lived with a partner at the time of his death, Angela. They had cohabited for three years.

Client is certain that Simon died without leaving a will.

Explained to client that there was the prospect of Angela claiming a sum against the estate and asked for more details.

## Assets and liabilities

James has a broad understanding of the estate but not a perfect one.

### Assets

- Simon owned his house with no mortgage, valued at approximately £200,000.
- Savings, stocks and shares amount to around £55,000.
- Total assets of £255,000.

### Liabilities

- Funeral costs and some credit card bills/unpaid debts = £5,000.

The overall value of the estate is therefore around £250,000.

Client is unaware of any pensions or life assurance policies.

In respect of inheritance tax: client was advised that, as the threshold for the tax is £325,000 and the current valuation is £250,000, it is unlikely that inheritance tax will be payable.

## Legal advice

Client was advised that because Simon died without a will the estate would follow intestacy rules. Explained that this had two relevant points on administration and distribution.

- For administration, letters of administration would be needed and someone would have to apply for these. Discussed whether client or sister would wish to do this and client agreed that he would.
- For distribution, client was advised of starting point: he and his sister would divide the estate between themselves equally once all liabilities had been paid.

However, client was advised that Angela could make a claim against the estate and seek a sum of money on the basis that she had lived with Simon for three years. She might be financially dependent on him, although there was not enough information to be certain of this.

Explained to client that Angela would have six months from the date that letters of administration were granted to make a claim. If she made a claim, this would be decided by the courts. The courts have great discretion here and would make an award that was seen to be just in all circumstances.

## Practical advice

Client was advised that there are limited options until it is known what Angela plans to do.

He should apply for letters of administration to be granted so that the six-month time frame starts.

He could wait to hear from Angela but he could also contact her, either himself or through our firm, to attempt to negotiate with her. This might save time and legal costs if she chooses to take legal action.

## Next steps – for the client

1.  Apply for letters of administration
2.  Consider whether he wants to contact Angela.

## Next steps – for the firm

1.  Send a client care letter to the client summarising advice.

---

## ATTENDANCE NOTE/LEGAL ANALYSIS
### Example 2: property

**Date:**    DD/MM/YYYY
**Time:**    10.00–10.25
**Client:**  Yusuf Ahmed
**Matter:**  Property dispute

Client attended to discuss a property matter with his neighbour (Klara Marks) about the boundaries between their lands.

Client is seeking to sell his property quickly and believes that he is entitled to a small amount of land that is owned by his neighbour. Client sought advice about his rights.

## The land

The client's property is a registered freehold property that he owns in his sole name.

Mortgage on the property of approximately £130,000.

Value of the property is approximately £210,000 – he has received an offer for £200,000. He has a back garden which adjoins his neighbour's back garden.

At the side of the client's garden is a small area (1.5 metres by 9 metres) before his neighbour's fence. For the past 15 years, the client has been using this to grow potatoes and onions. Klara Marks told him last month that this area was actually on her land according to the title plans. This has led to an argument and she has told him to stop using her land.

## Client's goals

The client is angry about the situation as he has looked after this land for 15 years. He wants to have the land officially with his property. However, he is keen to sell the property because he has a related purchase and he does not want that to fall through. The potential buyers for this property have commented on the vegetable patch and want to ensure that this is part of the land that is purchased. Client is concerned that the buyers may offer a lower price if it is not included.

## Legal advice

I advised the client that the starting point is the situation set out on the original title documents. Client believes that this means that the land belongs to his neighbour. Advised him that we can check this by reviewing the title documents with his property.

Advised client that there is the potential for a claim for adverse possession: if there is actual possession and client can demonstrate intention to possess then he can apply to have the land registered in his name because he has used the land for more than ten years without objection.

Client was advised that the test depends on the facts but there are some strong points:

- He has used the land consistently to grow vegetables, and that this has been for more than ten years.
- There is a fence between this land and his neighbour's garden, and it would appear to any passer-by to be part of his land.

Factually, there is a strong case to show that he has been in occupation for sufficient time.

However, client was advised that this does not mean he will succeed, and that he will need to apply to the Land Registry to be registered as the owner of this land. The neighbour can object, in which case he would have to show either:

1. that he was using the land in the mistaken but reasonable belief that he owned the land, or
2. that it would be unconscionable to leave the land in the neighbour's ownership.

For point 1, client admits he had not looked at the title deeds before using the land, and accepts that there was no confusion about the title boundary. Advice was that the mistake would not likely be seen as reasonable.

For point 2, client was advised that this was a possibility but a very high test to overcome. There are arguments but it was not possible to predict how the Land Registry would decide.

Client was advised that applying to the Land Registry would take time; then the neighbour would have 65 working days to respond. It could take up to 13 weeks from making the application to get a response from them before the Land Registry even have to consider it.

## Practical advice

Client was advised of the following options:

1. Do nothing and sell the property with an explanation of the disputed land – potentially lead to a reduced sale price.
2. Attempt to negotiate with the neighbour, possibly including a payment for the land to be officially transferred – no guarantee of success; could be time-consuming; there have been arguments between them.
3. Instruct the firm to negotiate with the neighbour on their behalf, rather than the client negotiating with the neighbour themselves.
4. Client (or the firm) applies to the Land Registry for adverse possession.

Client wanted time to consider, so I explained that I would send out a client care letter with full details and an estimate of costs.

## Next steps for client and the firm

1. Client care letter to be sent to client.
2. Client to provide the firm with title documents or instruct us to obtain.
3. If client proceeds, gather evidence about the use of the land.

### Attendance note/legal analysis technique

When compiling your summary of facts, if you are uncertain as to whether or not a fact should be included, think about its relevance to the case and the advice you gave to the client. You should only include facts that have a bearing on your legal analysis (remember the requirement under **AC 1** for the attendance note/legal analysis).

The crucial theme that runs through this part of the SQE2 assessment is clarity. You need to demonstrate to the assessor that you can provide a correct and clear record of your interview, and present the facts and your advice in a reader-friendly layout and style so that another reader would be able to pick up the file in the future and immediately understand the current situation of the case.

## ■ SUMMARY AND REFLECTION

You have now reached the end of the SQE2 client interview assessment. Bear in mind that you are allocated the same amount of time for writing the attendance note as for the client interview, which indicates the value of developing your skills for this aspect of the assessment.

Take time to review this chapter and understand how to demonstrate your competence under the specific assessment criteria for the attendance note/legal analysis:

- **AC 1**: include only the important and relevant facts that you gathered during the interview.
- **AC 2**: at the end of your attendance note, include the next steps for you and the client.
- **AC 3**: demonstrate in your note that you have focused your advice and legal analysis on the client's needs, goals and perspective, and your advice includes non-legal options.
- **AC 4**: your note must set out the correct legal principles for this matter and apply them to the client's case. Remember that this is different from the assessment criteria for the client interview itself, where you are *not* assessed on the accuracy of your legal advice. Your legal analysis *must* be correct for the attendance note.
- **AC 5**: your note must be sufficiently detailed and consider any ethical or professional conduct issues.

# 5

# Negotiation

Now that we have explored all aspects of the client interview assessment, including the preparation time beforehand, the interview itself and the attendance note, we turn to the specific skill of negotiation. None of the SQE2 oral or written skills assessments focuses solely on negotiation, but the SRA guidance on its website (sqe.sra.org.uk) states that 'all deliveries of SQE2 will contain at least one assessment involving negotiation'. At some point during your SQE2 assessments, you will therefore need to demonstrate an understanding of negotiation, and this chapter will help to develop your skills in this area.

Because there is not a separate assessment for negotiation, it is much harder to recommend methods of preparation. The SRA guidance simply states that negotiation could appear in three of your SQE2 assessments:

> Negotiation may be assessed in either interview and attendance note/legal analysis and/or case and matter analysis and/or legal writing.

The SQE2 assessment specification for 'Client interviewing and completion of attendance note/legal analysis' does not include negotiation in the client interview part of the assessment, only in the attendance note/legal analysis section:

> The attendance note/legal analysis should also identify the next steps to be taken by the solicitor and, where applicable, the client, as well as any ethical issues that arise and how they should be dealt with. This may (but will not necessarily) include options and strategies for negotiation.

You therefore need to have a working knowledge of negotiations: what the skill is, why it is important, and when it might appear in your SQE2 oral assessment. The Statement of Solicitor Competence that underpins the SQE2 assessment includes negotiations in skill B6. This gives a summary of the skills that you will need to understand and be able to demonstrate:

> B6. Negotiate solutions to clients' issues, including:
> • Identifying all parties' interests, objectives and limits.
> • Developing and formulating best options for meeting parties' objectives.
> • Presenting options for compromise persuasively.
> • Responding to options presented by the other side.
> • Developing compromises between options or parties.

All five of these competencies are reflected in the assessment criteria for client interviewing and also for attendance note/legal analysis, and we have already shown in Chapters 1 to 4 how you can demonstrate your competency at different stages of this oral assessment. In Chapters 3 and 4 we explained how you need to tailor options for the client that meet their objectives (**AC 4** for client interviewing, **AC 3** for attendance note). This will be explored further in this chapter, with a focus on negotiation as one of those options.

> ### Assessment technique
> Rather than thinking about negotiation as a separate skill, try to view it as integral to all of your SQE2 assessments. Be aware of what it is and when it might be appropriate so that you can, where appropriate, identify its potential relevance to the client's matter.

This chapter will examine the skill of negotiation from three aspects:

1. The importance of negotiation for a solicitor.
2. The merits of negotiation.
3. How to advise a client on negotiation.

# ■ THE IMPORTANCE OF NEGOTIATION FOR A SOLICITOR

## WHAT IS NEGOTIATION?

For the purpose of the SQE2 assessments, think about negotiation as simply a form of alternative dispute resolution (ADR): it is an attempt by at least two parties to resolve a matter that has arisen between them, through dialogue rather than litigation.

For example, imagine your neighbour is causing a nuisance by playing music loudly at night:

- One option might be to issue legal proceedings against them. This might stop the nuisance but it is a costly and time-consuming process, and would create bad feeling between you and the neighbour.
- An alternative would be to seek to negotiate with them. You could express your concerns and try to reach a compromise, such as agreeing that the neighbour will play the music at an agreed volume and only between certain hours.

## THE DIFFERENCE BETWEEN NEGOTIATION AND MEDIATION

Mediation is another form of ADR, and it can sometimes be confused with negotiation. During mediation, the parties in dispute come together, with or without legal representatives, to discuss the matter with each other and a neutral third party: the mediator.

Informal mediations frequently take place in everyday life. For example, in a situation where two tenants of a house are constantly arguing, a third tenant might be the one who helps to bring the other two closer together to resolve the issues. This person is essentially performing the same function as a formal mediator.

The mediator is not there to determine who has the stronger argument or who should win the case, and the mediator's fees are normally paid equally by the parties to avoid any allegation of favouritism or bias. Their role is to:

- facilitate the resolution of the dispute
- help to build a bridge between the parties
- address the emotions of the situation
- bring the parties closer together from their often extreme positions.

The mediator does not compel a resolution, and even if the mediation does not produce a complete settlement, the aim is to bring the parties closer to reaching an agreement at a later date.

Mediation is not specifically mentioned in the SRA guidelines, and so it is not something that you will be assessed on. However, mediation has been growing in popularity over the past three decades, and in 2023 the government announced the results of a consultation on 'Increasing the use of mediation in the civil justice system'. In summary, the consultation process found that mediation was a favourable means of dealing with civil disputes. As a result, the government announced plans to compel the use of mediation for disputes with a financial value below £10,000. On 22 May 2024 the Civil Procedure Rules were amended (Practice Direction 51ZE) to state that in all cases under £10,000 the parties would automatically be referred to the small courts mediation service. Although it is not compulsory for the parties to attend these, there is an expectation that they should, and the courts retain powers to issue costs orders in the event of ADR not being pursued. As this is an evolving discussion, it is important to keep an eye on developments to ensure that you give the appropriate advice.

The crucial point is that alternatives to litigation are preferable. When advising a client, particularly in a contentious case, the potential suitability for negotiation and/or mediation is something that you should always consider.

# ■ THE MERITS OF NEGOTIATION

There are many advantages and some disadvantages to negotiation. You might be required to identify and explain these to the client in your SQE2 skills assessments, both in the written skills assessments for case and matter analysis and legal writing and in the attendance note portion of the client interview assessment.

## POTENTIAL ADVANTAGES OF NEGOTIATIONS FOR A CLIENT

As we have already seen from our examples above, the key advantage of negotiation is that it can provide solutions that:

- address the specific concerns of the client
- can be produced quickly
- are cost-efficient
- involve the other party.

Let's explore each of these advantages in turn.

### Address the specific concerns of the client

Claims brought by the claimant in a dispute often do not reflect what the client wants but what they have (correctly) been advised they are able to claim. These remedies are limited: the court can order financial compensation to be paid and, in certain circumstances, can issue injunctions to require someone to do an act or refrain from doing it. These remedies may serve a purpose and bring satisfaction to the client but they might only have pursued litigation because it was available, not because they actually wanted to pursue this option.

For example, consider a neighbourhood dispute where your client feels that their neighbour has been deliberately doing an act to aggravate them. They have suffered no financial loss but the situation has led to high emotions, and what the client really wants is an apology. This is not something that the courts can compel but it can be agreed in a negotiation. As well as meeting the client's objectives (a competency required under **AC 3** for the attendance note), this might also benefit the neighbour as it is likely to be cheaper than the process for claiming potential damages or issuing an injunction.

## Quicker results

Although you should not fall into the trap of reassuring the client that negotiation will automatically resolve the matter quickly as every dispute is unique, it is safe to advise them that entering the process of negotiations is speedier than litigation.

Save for emergency situations, the Civil Procedure Rules require a long process of pre-action steps that must be taken before issuing legal proceedings, which then enter the court system, from which it can take a long time to reach a final hearing, even in comparatively straightforward cases. You would need to make the client aware of this potential for delay, so that they can make an informed decision about their options (managing client expectations is a competency you need to demonstrate under **AC 5** of the client interview).

By contrast, you could advise the client that, although first you need to comply with the relevant pre-action steps and so on, you might be able to achieve a swifter resolution by instigating negotiations with the other party, such as writing a letter to them or arranging a conversation with them or their solicitor. You could advise that the client themselves write or arrange the conversation, which might be even quicker. Such actions are a long way from reaching a satisfactory conclusion, but there is at least the potential for the matter to resolve itself far quicker than entering the court process.

### Example 2: property

Yusuf may have the chance of success after a long litigation process but he needs a quick sale. Therefore, negotiating with his neighbour may be a preferable option for him, and one that he should be advised to consider.

## Cost-efficiency

Negotiation is generally cheaper than litigation. Bear in mind that there will still be some costs, such as paying for a solicitor's time to deal with the negotiation, and we would caution you against describing it to a client in your SQE2 assessment as a 'cheap' option. However, it can be said with certainty that negotiation is cost-effective, and by negotiating the client can explore the potential for resolution at a relatively small cost. It allows them to avoid the higher costs of a case running all the way to trial, so you should always consider whether negotiation is a viable option and in your client's best interests (to reiterate Principle 7 of the SRA Code of Conduct 2019). This should not be suggested as a default simply because it is cheaper and faster – it has to be appropriate in the circumstances.

### Example 1: wills and probate

The starting point was that James and his sister would be able to claim equal shares of the estate but that Simon's partner Angela had a potential claim against the estate on the grounds that she had not been reasonably provided for. When forming your advice on this aspect of the case, you would need to inform the client that, although this matter could be resolved by the court, the parties could, conceivably, negotiate a settlement to avoid the costs and time of litigation.

## Involve the opponent

During a negotiated agreement, the client's opponent is seen as part of the *solution* rather than part of the *problem*. There are some situations where this can be crucial. For example, in the example on page 68 where the client is considering whether or not to sue their neighbour, you would need to discuss their continuing relationship after the resolution of the case. It would be useful to ask the client what they would like that relationship to be, and how this might be affected by a long-drawn-out course of litigation. Even if the client wins the case and achieves their initial objective, it is unlikely that their relationship with the neighbour will be sustainable. This outcome might not be in the client's best interest.

Although unlikely to be the subject of your SQE2 client interview assessment, the same principle applies to professional and working relationships: litigation is unlikely to assist with long-term relationships.

By contrast, involving the client's opponent in the process allows you to help them understand matters from your client's perspective, and enables them to be part of the process:

- If the neighbour voluntarily agrees not to play music past a particular time, then there is more likely to be an understanding between them and your client, and the potential for give and take in the future.
- If on the other hand the neighbour is ordered by a court not to play music past a certain hour, they are likely to feel frustration and anger, and this could easily lead to a fresh dispute in the future.

## NEGOTIATION IS NOT ALWAYS THE ANSWER!

Although negotiations and ADR can be attractive options that you would want to advise your client to consider, remember that the SQE2 assessment criteria requires you to maintain a client-focused approach. It is particularly important in the SQE2 client interview assessment to ensure, as discussed in Chapter 3, that you present bespoke options for the client rather than a generic list. Whilst there are advantages to negotiation in many situations, and you might want to recommend entering negotiations in your attendance note, there are also potential drawbacks and times when negotiation is not appropriate. For example:

- Drawback: no resolution is reached.
- Not appropriate: the issue is time-sensitive.

You need to think carefully about the information provided by the SQE2 assessment materials and the client during the interview, and consider whether or not negotiation is the best option.

### No resolution is reached

One of the advantages of negotiation as discussed above is that it can be a quicker process than litigation. However, crucially, an advantage of litigation is that you do get a result (eventually). You have a definitive answer, and you have either won or lost the case. The same cannot be said for negotiation: there is no end date to the resolution, and negotiation has the potential to draw out the process even longer than waiting for a court judgement.

For example:

- If litigation will take two years but negotiation takes two months, it is quicker to negotiate than to litigate.
- However, if the negotiation fails and the client then chooses to take the litigation route, then negotiating has increased the time to two years and two months.

This does not mean that the negotiation period was wasted or that it was a poor idea, but it is important to remember that, because negotiations will only succeed if the other side agrees (1) to sit down and negotiate and (2) to resolve the matter, it is possible for negotiation to make the process longer.

### The issue is time-sensitive

Negotiation might not be the best option when the client's issue is particularly time-sensitive. For example, if a landlord has threatened to evict your client at 9 AM the following day, the clear priority will be to issue legal proceedings for an emergency injunction. Only after that has been achieved will you advise on the possibility of negotiation.

> **Assessment technique**
>
> When framing your advice and particularly when considering different options such as negotiations, think carefully about how it might impact on this client and their case.

## THE IMPORTANCE OF UNDERSTANDING THE CLIENT'S OBJECTIVES, NEEDS AND INTERESTS

Understanding the objective of the client is normally quite straightforward. You will discover what the client wants to achieve by reading the SQE2 assessment materials and asking a combination of open and closed questions in the interview, as we explored in Chapter 2. Understanding the needs or interests of the client can be more difficult, but this provides an entry point to more creative options such as negotiation that can benefit the client.

Let's continue the example of the neighbour dispute over noise outlined on page 68:

1.  You could start to compose your legal advice based on the client's wish to issue proceedings against their neighbour because of the regular, intolerable noise of their music at night. You could advise the client that you will address pre-action protocols and, if necessary, pursue the case through the courts to resolution.
2.  To fully advise the client, however, you would need to go beyond this position to consider what the needs of the client might be in this situation. Whether these needs make the position stronger or weaker for the client is not the crucial issue – the key is that knowing about them will give you a better understanding of what will benefit the client. In this example, the client might want the noise to stop because it is disturbing their sleep, they have a nervous disposition and a stressful job, and the situation is causing the client to underperform at work.

    Apart from simply having more information, uncovering the needs of the client has widened your ability to give advice and has added a cautionary note. Your preliminary advice, based on the client's position alone, might have been to issue legal proceedings. Understanding that the client is of a nervous disposition and has a stressful job might however lead you to consider whether a potentially protracted claim through the courts, in which they would have to relive the incidents when giving evidence and be subjected to cross-examination, is necessarily in their best interests.
3.  The next step would be to reflect on whether the needs of the client mean that alternative options should be explored. The client's primary objective is to stop the loud music at night and to regain their equilibrium at work. You might then consider whether a negotiation with the neighbour might be a preferable solution to this problem. It would potentially lead to a speedier resolution, it avoids court action, and it could be achieved by you and the neighbour's solicitor without any presence or direct action by the client, if that is what they wish.

During the interview you might also uncover additional potential needs and interests that could persuade you to advise negotiation. In a neighbour dispute, these could be:

• the need for a continuing relationship with a neighbour
• the reaction of other people in the neighbourhood.

Your open and closed questions might reveal that the client cannot afford to move and therefore wants to retain a positive, or at worst neutral, relationship with the neighbour. This would move litigation further down the list of possible options, rather than being the first option when considering the client's legal position.

If, having discovered further context/background for the client's issue, you decide to advise them to enter negotiation, remember that now you must consider the other party's perspective. Negotiation is, by definition, a multiparty process and if the other party is not prepared to negotiate then this is not a viable course of action to recommend.

Inevitably it will be more difficult to find out what the needs and interests of the other party might be. In an SQE2 assessment you would try to find out more about the neighbour by asking the client further closed questions, and work out whether it is sensible to suggest negotiation as a possible avenue to resolve the issue.

The neighbour's *position* is that they are playing loud music at the stated times. To discover the *needs/interests* of the neighbour, you would need to consider the reasons behind their choice to play music late at night. The client might be able to give some insights, and you would try to tease out the reasons by considering the following possibilities:

• Does the neighbour work night shifts, and for them the early hours of the morning are, effectively, the middle of the day and not the middle of the night?
• Is your neighbour definitely the person playing the music, or could someone else in the house be doing so?
• Does the neighbour have any reason to be accidently playing the music loudly?

Although it could transpire that none of these possibilities is close to the truth, speculating on the neighbour's needs or interests brings more nuance to the case. It allows the client to consider reasons for the loud music other than the neighbour just trying to annoy them. Starting to consider the other party's point of view is strong preparation for an eventual negotiation.

## ■ HOW TO ADVISE A CLIENT ON NEGOTIATION

When considering whether negotiation is a logical option to propose to the client, these three stages could form a useful checklist for you to work through in the SQE2 assessment:

• Explore whether negotiation is a viable option for the client in this situation.
• Explain to the client how negotiation works, and the advantages/disadvantages of different types.
• Form objective, client-focused advice on negotiation.

### EXPLORE THE VIABILITY OF NEGOTIATION

The SQE2 client interview assessment focuses on two areas of law: wills/probate and property. Of these two, it is the property interview in which you will be most likely to consider negotiation, because property tends to involve an active relationship with another person and, conceivably, a conflict. There will, however, be opportunities in the wills and probate interview, such as when a party wants to claim for additional provision under the existing will.

---

**Example 1: wills and probate**

You have found out that there is a potential claim from Angela, the partner of the deceased. Whilst there is no certainty that a claim will be made against the estate, it would be appropriate to advise your client that, if a claim is made, the administrators of the estate may negotiate with Angela in order to resolve the matter without going to court, and that this may be cheaper and quicker in the long run in order to allow the estate to be finalised.

---

Negotiation in the property interview could involve discussions about:

- additional chattels that the client wishes to purchase in a conveyance
- purchasing lands or rights to easements.

If the issue involves a conflict, resolving that conflict by way of a negotiation will always be a viable option.

---

**Example 2: property**

As we mentioned in Chapter 4, it would certainly be appropriate to advise Yusuf to negotiate with his neighbour over ownership of the strip of land. This would avoid a time-consuming application to the Land Registry, which would delay the sale of his property. Also, your legal analysis will have led you to realise that, although Yusuf has a possible case under adverse possession, it is not watertight, and negotiation might be the best option for him to achieve his goals.

---

## EXPLAIN TO THE CLIENT HOW NEGOTIATION WORKS

You might assume that the client knows exactly what a negotiation is, but it is still important to explain the concept to so that you are sure that they understand the process. The easiest way to do this is to break down how it would work in practice; that is, that either you and/or the client would sit down and discuss the situation with the other party, with a view to finding a way to resolve the situation together.

You need to explain the different types of negotiation, particularly as they each have advantages and disadvantages that could apply to your client. The different types of negotiation are:

- The client negotiates directly with the other side.
- The client instructs the solicitor to negotiate with the other side.

### The client negotiates directly with the other side

The most cost-effective way is simply for the client to contact the other side and ask to talk about the situation, possibly without even using the term 'negotiation'. The obvious advantages to this are:

- It is cheap, at least in respect of the solicitor's costs.
- The client can retain the personal touch.
- The risk of solicitor-escalation can be avoided – as soon as a solicitor's letter is received by the other party, they might feel defensive about the conflict becoming more formal and official.

Disadvantages of this form of negotiation include the following:

- The client might not be confident in approaching the other party in a dispute, particularly if they feel upset about the situation.
- The client might feel that they would not be taken as seriously as a solicitor making suggestions.

Nonetheless, negotiation might remain the preferred option, particularly if the client does not have significant financial resources to pursue litigation.

### The client instructs the solicitor to negotiate with the other side

The alternative is for the solicitor to propose a meeting to discuss and negotiate the situation, with either the other side in person or, more likely, their legal representative.

The advantages of this option are:

- The solicitor will be at arm's length from emotive elements of the dispute, and is less likely to be distracted by those emotions.
- Formal discussions will take place, with the potential of future legal action if the negotiations fail.

The potential drawbacks here are, effectively, the flipside of the advantages of the first option, the client negotiating with the other party:

- This type of negotiation loses the personal touch, as it necessarily becomes a more formal proceeding.
- Instructing a solicitor to negotiate on the client's behalf will incur costs, which could be prohibitive for the client.

However, this type of negotiation will often be the client's choice, and they might especially prefer their solicitor to engage with the other side if there are already signs of conflict.

## FORM OBJECTIVE, CLIENT-FOCUSED ADVICE

You must maintain a client-focused approach when forming advice on negotiation, as emphasised in the SQE2 assessment criteria. In particular, criterion B3 on the SRA website states that candidates must:

> Develop and advise on relevant options, strategies and solutions, including:
> a) Understanding and assessing a client's commercial and personal circumstances, their needs, objectives, priorities and constraints.
> b) Ensuring that advice is informed by appropriate legal and factual analysis and identifies the consequences of different options.

Our suggestions for forming advice on negotiation are as follows:

1. Keep it simple! Explain that you will be following up the interview with a letter of advice, confirming discussions and decisions made during the interview. However, the client might want to know some specific details before leaving the interview. If they are concerned about the cost of options (including both negotiation and court action), you do not have to give a precise estimate but you could refer to the firm's customer care letter, which would include your hourly rate, and explain briefly what the negotiation might involve in terms of time.

2.  Focus on the main points. There will be advantages and disadvantages to all the options but some will be more pronounced than others. For example, a clear disadvantage is that you cannot guarantee that negotiation will work as it depends on the other side's cooperation. You need to make this clear to the client to ensure that you manage their expectations, an important aspect of maintaining an effective relationship with the client as specified by **AC 5** for the client interview.
3.  Do not let your own preference cloud your advice. At the heart of this assessment is the client's concern about their issue, and, even though you might think that it is the perfect case for a negotiation, make sure that you are not pushing the client towards a choice that they do not want to make.

# ■ SUMMARY AND REFLECTION

Negotiation is an important part of legal practice and, with litigation becoming ever more time-consuming, the attraction of ADR options will only increase. For the purposes of the SQE2 assessments, however, the important thing for you to do is to:

- identify when advising on negotiation might be relevant
- consider this option from the client's perspective.

Including negotiation as an option for next steps in your attendance note provides an excellent opportunity to demonstrate your ability to be client-focused in your advice, as required by the SRA's **AC 3** for attendance note/legal analysis. Make sure you understand how to identify whether it is appropriate in the circumstances and are able to justify that opinion.

# 6

# Interview skills in practice

Chapters 1 to 5 have covered the different elements of the SQE2 client interview assessment, exploring techniques and approaches that we hope will help you to develop confidence and an excellent set of skills for this important aspect of solicitor practice.

This chapter will draw together our guidance from these previous chapters and provide examples of different approaches in the context of **Example 1: wills and probate** and **Example 2: property** as set out in the introduction. We will explore good practice for these parts of the interview:

1. Read the assessment materials.
2. Gather information.
3. Test the client's case.
4. Summarise and understand your client's priorities.
5. Provide advice that gives the client an informed choice.
6. Build a professional relationship.
7. Apply the law.
8. Conclude the interview.

We invite you to 'have a go' at considering the strengths or weaknesses of each sample response. A commentary will then highlight the elements that create a successful response and also explain how poorer responses would fail to prove a candidate's competency as specified in the SQE2 assessment criteria for client interviewing. This is important for your preparation for SQE2, because the assessment is not a memory test: you will need to apply your skills to the context of the client that you are interviewing and hold the assessment criteria in your mind at all times. Here is a reminder of the assessment criteria for client interviewing:

---

**SQE2 client interviewing assessment criteria**

**Skills**

1. Listen to the client and use questioning effectively to enable the client to tell the solicitor what is important to them.
2. Communicate and explain in a way that is suitable for the client to understand.
3. Conduct themselves in a professional manner and treat the client with courtesy, respect and politeness including respecting diversity where relevant.
4. Demonstrate client-focus in their approach to the client and the issues (ie demonstrate an understanding of the problem from the client's point of view and what the client wants to achieve, not just from a legal perspective).
5. Establish and maintain an effective relationship with the client so as to build trust and confidence.

---

Remember also that the SRA's performance indicators for each client interviewing assessment criterion are included in the Appendix.

# ■ READ THE ASSESSMENT MATERIALS

Let's remind ourselves of **Example 2: property** from the introduction:

---

### Example 2: property

Yusuf Ahmed has come to see you regarding a potential dispute with his neighbour, Klara Marks. He believes that he has a right to own part of his neighbour's land and wants to know what he can do about it before he sells the property. Both his land and his neighbour's land are registered.

---

This paragraph could be a snippet from a longer SQE2 question. Although it is brief, it contains important information about the client's legal issue that you could glean during the ten-minute preparation time:

1. **The registration status of the relevant land**.
   You are told that all relevant land is registered.
   - You could confirm this again with the client in the early stages of the interview, but this is a helpful starting point because it indicates the direction that the interview might take.
   - You know that there will be Land Registry documents but you do not know if the client will have them to hand. It will be important to ask whether the client has all available documents in their possession.
2. **The nature of the client's claim: the right to neighbour's land**.
   The information suggests that the dispute is likely to concern land that Yusuf believes he is entitled to, and that land appears to be owned by the neighbour.
   - This narrows down the options considerably, and should bring the topics of adverse possession, easements, covenants and boundary dispute principles to the forefront of your mind.
   - When you connect this point to the land being registered, you can start to think about the focus of your questions, such as: does the title document set out a right (whether by easement or covenant)? With respect to adverse possession, how long has the client used the land for?
3. **The nature of the issue – adverse possession**.
   You have been told that the client believes that his neighbour's land belongs to him.
   - This is likely to involve an element of hostile action, which means that your advice could involve litigation, whether through the courts or through an application to the Land Registry.
   - As the client wants to sell the property, you should be thinking of practical considerations too: how long would litigation hold up a sale? How important is the sale to the client?
   - Although litigation might be an obvious option, you are also told that the other party is a neighbour. This factor, linked to the need to sell, means that negotiation might be a possible option later in the interview.

---

### Assessment technique

Always read the SQE2 memorandum carefully. Even a short paragraph could provide you with important information. Sometimes the issue will be obvious, and at other times the memo might prompt you to think of the relevant questions to ask in the interview.

---

# ■ GATHER INFORMATION

If you can only glean little information from the SQE2 assessment memorandum, information-gathering will be even more important in stage 2 of the interview (as explored in Chapter 2). You will need to obtain further information from your client before you are in a position to provide advice. Draw on the method of questioning described in Chapter 2, beginning with open, broader questions and then moving on to closed questions to request specific details.

Try to link a piece of information that you gained about the case during the ten-minute preparation time to your first question.

## HAVE A GO

Take a look at these examples of opening questions and decide which is the stronger question.

**A** I understand from the memorandum that your neighbour has land that you believe is yours. Can you explain this in more detail?

**B** Please could you tell me why you are here today?

## COMMENTARY

Example A is more tailored to the specific client. It shows the client that you have read the email and understand the subject of the case, whilst confirming in a clear and appropriate fashion that you need more detail.

Example B is weaker as an opening question, because it gives the impression that you have not processed information contained in the memorandum that you received, or that you have not read it. The manner is also more abrupt (try to say both questions out loud, and you should hear a clear distinction between them). The question is not ineffective, as it does cover what you want to achieve – find out why the client wants advice – but this approach is not conducive to a professional relationship.

The client will probably respond to your opening question by providing additional information about their reasons for seeing you.

### Assessment technique

Remember that one of the drawbacks of an open question is that you lose some element of control over the interview as you are inviting the client to talk freely. You might also gain some irrelevant information, and it is important that you trust your judgement to discern what is important to the case.

The client's response should clarify the legal issue significantly.

### Example 2: property

Yusuf might respond by saying that he has been using a strip of land on the boundary between his property and that of his neighbours, and he has read somewhere that this means that it now belongs to him.

Once the client has answered, you can choose other open questions – such as:

> Can you tell me more?

> Can you help me understand the situation more fully?

Alternatively, you might move straight to closed questions. There is no right or wrong answer here but do consider whether another open question will provide any more information.

By this point you should have identified that the client is interested in adverse possession, although he is not likely to have used this phrase. Your FLK preparation on the subject matter should alert you to several points on which you need further information. Specifically, in order to advise on whether adverse possession has been established, you will need to know:

- how long the land has been used for (to meet the time requirements)
- how the land has been used (to determine whether actual possession has been satisfied)
- whether Yusuf's actions were with permission of the neighbour (to determine if the neighbour is adverse)
- the situation with selling the property (do not forget the memorandum!)
- what the relationship is like with the neighbour (always a useful question).

## Assessment technique

When preparing for this assessment it is important to understand the components for each of the possible topics that can be used in the assessment. It is equally important, however, to know how you can get that information. When preparing ahead of the assessment day, you should think about not only what the legal tests are but also what information you need to gain from the client in order to evaluate those tests. Unlike a problem question, the relevant information will not simply be laid out for you.

How you approach these questions is your choice but it is important to remain focused on a particular area so that the client can understand the direction in which you are taking the interview. Moving from one topic to another can confuse the client and lead to uncertainty in their answers.

## HAVE A GO

You have asked the initial question:

> Your email suggested you were selling the property. Can you tell me more about that?

Now decide which of these sets of follow-up questions is the most successful:

**A** > How long have you used the land for?

> How much is it on the market for?

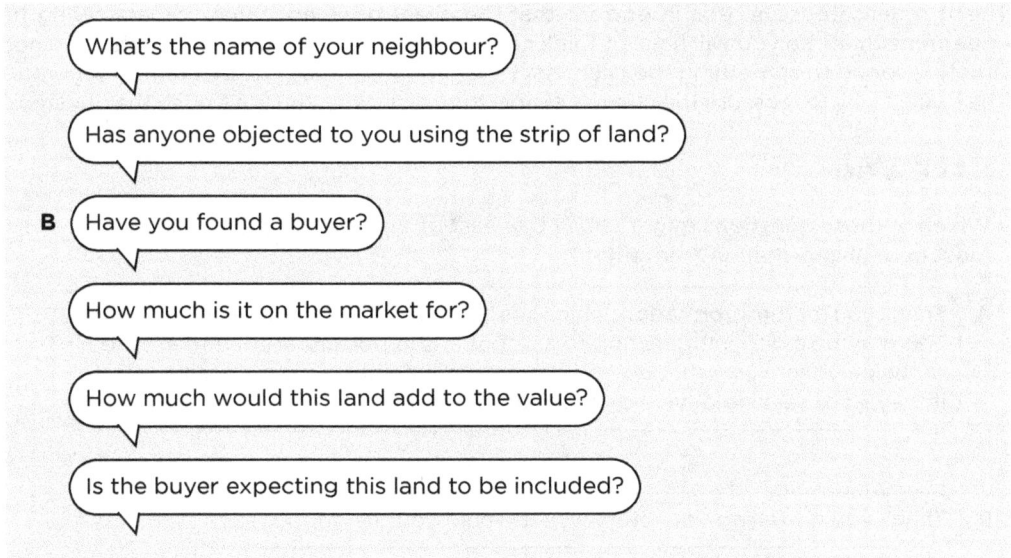

> What's the name of your neighbour?

> Has anyone objected to you using the strip of land?

**B** Have you found a buyer?

> How much is it on the market for?

> How much would this land add to the value?

> Is the buyer expecting this land to be included?

## COMMENTARY

The questions in Example A are not necessarily poor, and they will generate the information that you need, but they are presented in a confused order and risk causing confusion and hesitation for the client. Two analogies can assist here:

- This approach is likely to be seen more as an interrogation than a friendly conversation. This type of questioning is sometimes used in criminal law, as a tactic in cross-examination to undermine the credibility of the witness. In a client interview, such an outcome is clearly undesirable.
- Imagine that you are meeting a friend and you ask them questions about their job, their family and their hobby in quick succession. The natural flow of information and conversation will be disturbed and you are less likely to gain a full picture of any topic.

By contrast, the questions in Example B follow a logical order and progression. The client can understand the direction of your questioning and will be more relaxed and cooperative in answering you.

### Interview technique

Try to deal with one topic at a time. If you have ascertained that you need information on five points, group your questions around the first point, then the second, and so on until you have addressed all five points.

Deciding which point to start with is a matter of preference: you could begin by asking about what you consider to be the most important matter, or the question that will be easiest for the client to answer.

You could follow this pattern for the remainder of the information-gathering stage. It is useful to signal to the client when your questions are moving on to another topic.

## ■ TEST THE CLIENT'S CASE

The client will give you their version of events, naturally based on their own perspective. In order to provide objective advice to your client, you need to develop a fuller picture of the situation, which includes the view of the other party.

This is a delicate issue. It is important that the client does not think you are trying to undermine them, so you will have to think carefully about how you approach this and not simply respond to something the client says that you think may not be entirely accurate. The easiest way to reassure the client is simply to explain why you are asking the question.

## HAVE A GO

Which of these questions might cause the least offence to the client, and extract the most helpful information from them?

**A** Thank you for the information, which has helped me to understand the situation. This may be a difficult question to ask, but it is important that I understand all of the perspectives. What do you imagine your neighbour would tell a solicitor if they were seeking advice on this matter?

**B** Thank you for telling your story. What would your neighbour say?

## COMMENTARY

Example B, on its face, looks perfectly reasonable. However, there are a number of weaknesses:

- The word 'story' is commonly associated with fiction, and, even if it is not meant to have that connotation, there is a danger that your client will see it as criticism of their perspective. Try to avoid using this word.
- The client is seeking advice from you and they might not understand why you are focusing on the other side.

This question might not elicit a negative response from the client but always consider how the client might interpret your words from the most negative angle.

By contrast, Example A affirms the importance attached to the client's words and explains why you are about to ask a challenging question. The client may still not like your question but you have provided appropriate context.

Explaining why you are asking something can be effective in many situations, including when you are asking for personal or sensitive information. For example:

- In a wills and probate interview you might need to ask about the client's relationship with a sibling or other relative.
- In a property interview you might ask whether there have been any incidents in the past with a neighbour.

However you approach this particular situation, it is vital that you consider the possibility that the client might not be telling you everything about the situation: there are two sides to every tale and your job is to build the most complete picture of events that you can.

## ■ SUMMARISE AND UNDERSTAND YOUR CLIENT'S PRIORITIES

As explained in Chapter 2, when you have finished gathering information from the client, you should summarise their position so that you can be certain that the details are accurate and that the client can be confident that you fully understand their position. It is also an excellent opportunity for the client to correct any errors (which will occasionally happen) and for you to ensure that you have an accurate chronology of events. This can be difficult when there is a vast array of information at your disposal, so we recommend the following:

- Try to focus on the most relevant information and the objectives of the client in the summary.
- Do not simply repeat what the client has told you; this adds nothing and will simply waste precious time.

### Interview technique

Remember our guidance from Chapter 2: think about how you take notes when listening to the client. Taking a verbatim note is unlikely to assist as you will spend most of your time writing rather than listening to the client. However, if you take clear (and legible!) notes of the important points that you have heard (including dates) it will be much easier to summarise the information.

## HAVE A GO

Below are two summaries, which assume that further information has been given during the client interview in **Example 2: property**. Read through these summaries and decide which would provide the candidate with the strongest platform for entering the advice-giving stage of the interview:

A    Yusuf, you are currently selling your property and have a potential buyer, who has made an offer on your home of £200,000. They have said that they want to include in the purchase a strip of land at the bottom part of your garden. You believe that this land is owned by your neighbour, Klara, and want to know if there is any way of moving it to your ownership. You have used this land for the past 15 years to grow fruit and vegetables on a regular basis, and have never had any objection from Klara. You regularly tend to the area during the day, particularly during the summer. You have spoken to Klara and she says that it is her land and has no interest in selling it. You are not sure how much the property would be worth without the land but are concerned that the buyer might pull out if it is not included. Your main goal is to sell the property because you have a related purchase. Is that an accurate summary of the situation?

B    Yusuf, you are concerned about land that is currently owned by Klara but you think it should belong to you because you have used it for a long period of time. Klara doesn't want to let you have your land and this might add some value to your property and this is important because you want to sell the land. Oh, and you have used it to grow some things on over the past, well, at least 12 years, I think you said.

## COMMENTARY

Example A is effective for three reasons:

- It is concise and should not take too much time to deliver.
- It summarises the crucial points from the information gathered from the client.
- It refers to the client's goals and targets.

Example B is less effective because it is imprecise and at times inaccurate. There is a lack of clear structure and a degree of uncertainty, which will cause the client to lose confidence in the advice that you have provided.

## ■ PROVIDE ADVICE THAT GIVES THE CLIENT AN INFORMED CHOICE

When forming your advice to the client, you need to make sure that they understand the different options and feel empowered to make an informed choice. This can be difficult to prepare for, because the options will depend on exactly what the client wants to achieve or, more accurately, what they believe they want to achieve. There will be some common advantages and disadvantages: litigation will always be potentially time-consuming and expensive, whilst negotiation will generally be a quicker process but lacks a certain resolution. However, as we have discussed throughout this book, you must tailor your advice to the client rather than relying on general legal principles, and provide advantages and disadvantages for all other options.

### HAVE A GO

Consider the scenario in **Example 2: property** again. Which of these examples of advice focuses on the client's perspective and allows them to make an informed choice?

A — Your best option is to let this drop. You have a claim to the land but it would need an application to the Land Registry, which the neighbour will contest. It will take a very long time, so my advice for you is to stop pursuing a claim to this land, sell the property without it and leave this issue for the buyer to sort out.

B — I have just set out the legal position for you. Now I am going to explain the various options that you have. I will explain the advantages and the disadvantages for each one, and set out what they might involve. I must stress that the choice is entirely yours. If you have any questions, please do ask.

Your first option is to try to enforce your rights over the land and have it transferred to your title. To do this you would need to make an application to the Land Registry with the evidence that we talked about a moment ago when discussing your legal position. If your neighbour doesn't respond then it will be registered in your name. If they object then it will take longer because the Land Registry will have to decide whether or not the land should be transferred.

The advantages to this are ... [*certainty and the long-term gains*].

The disadvantages to this are ... [*the time it would take to succeed if there is opposition, and even if there isn't, the potential costs of a drawn-out application, and the risk of losing the sale*].

## COMMENTARY

Example B sets out one viable option and lists its advantages and disadvantages. It does not push the client towards this particular option and it emphasises that they are free to make their own decision. In an SQE2 assessment you would then repeat this process for other options, which for this scenario could include:

- the client negotiating with the neighbour to agree to the process
- the firm negotiating on their behalf
- the client accepting that they cannot own the land and proceeding with the sale without the land.

By contrast, Example A is an extreme example of the client not being provided with an informed choice. Taking such an approach can be tempting as it pushes the client towards the path that you are likely to be drawn towards and brings the matter to a swift resolution. However, it contains a number of issues that weaken the quality of the advice:

- It is too short and therefore the options are not developed; there is no consideration of the advantages or disadvantages, or even an indication of what they involve. The client will be unable to make an informed decision on the best path forward.
- The options are merged into one, because of the speed with which they were delivered. The implication is that the client only has one option, emphasised by 'your best option'.

The approach in Example A is contrary to the entire thrust of the SQE2 assessment criteria, with its emphasis on listening to the client's concerns and focusing on what they want to achieve.

### Assessment technique

Remember that the correct advice might not necessarily be what the client wants or was expecting to hear! However, you are bound by the Principle 7 of the SRA Code of Conduct 2019 to act in the client's best interests, and SQE2 **AC 3** for client interviewing requires you to be able to deliver difficult or unwelcome news with sensitivity. This is an opportunity for you to demonstrate your professional manner with the client, which will help to gain their trust and confidence (and so achieve **AC 5**, establish and maintain an effective relationship with the client).

## ■ BUILD A PROFESSIONAL RELATIONSHIP

We will turn to **Example 1: wills and probate** to explore the remaining points of good practice in this chapter. A reminder of the details:

### Example 1: wills and probate

James Smith has come to see you for advice regarding his father Simon's estate. Simon died earlier this month. He had not made a will at the time of his death and therefore died intestate. At the time of his father's death, Simon was divorced and had two living children, James and Lucy. He was living with his partner, Angela.

You should anticipate that any wills and probate interview will involve a client who has lost someone close to them. You need to keep this in your thoughts at all times. It is a professional setting but you also need to be aware of the emotions that a client may be experiencing in the interview, and this is most prominent here, even with an assessor actor playing the role of client during the SQE2 assessment. To demonstrate sensitivity and respect for the client's situation and develop your professional relationship with them, we recommend the following:

- Read the memorandum carefully to make sure that you have understood the correct details (including who has died and, in this case, the relation of the client to the deceased).
- Listen closely to what the client says so that you do not respond to their answer with an insensitive follow-up question or one that implies that you are not empathising with them.

## HAVE A GO

Consider the following conversations between a candidate and client. Which one demonstrates sensitivity and empathy with the client, and is most likely to help the candidate develop a rapport with them?

**A**  Candidate:  What brings you here today?

   Client:  Well, my father died.

   Candidate:  I see, and what is it you would like to do?

**B**  Candidate:  I understand that you are here to discuss a situation regarding your father, who passed away recently. First, please accept my condolences for your loss.

   Client:  Thank you. I appreciate that.

   Candidate:  I can imagine that some of the topics we discuss today may be difficult for you. If you need to take a minute, don't hesitate to tell me.

## COMMENTARY

There is a clear difference between these two examples.

In Example B, the candidate has immediately demonstrated that they have read the memorandum and understand the situation. They then empathise with the client and show concern for their feelings, which will help to set a strong foundation for the interview and the professional relationship that will follow.

It is equally clear why Example A is weak:

- The candidate should know why the client has come in because this is stated in the memorandum (as it would be in an SQE2 assessment memorandum).
- The candidate has reacted thoughtlessly to what the client said, without listening and reacting appropriately. This will damage their relationship and rapport with the client.

## ■ APPLY THE LAW

The way that you apply the law to the client's situation in the SQE2 client interview assessment will probably be different in the two interviews. The property interview will usually focus on one central issue, such as adverse possession, easements or boundary disputes, perhaps including subsets of that core issue. In the wills and probate interview, you might need to discuss a range of separate, smaller issues, all with their own legal position. The client might need to be advised on the primary residue, anything that falls outside the will itself, and a list of specific bequests. In addition, they might have additional concerns including inheritance tax and the potential for further claims against the estate, either on their behalf or by someone else that may impact upon their legacy.

It is important that you have a clear structure, so that you can be confident of advising the client on both the general points of concern and the specific issues. Remind yourself of our advice on structure in Chapter 3. You can choose whichever structure best suits your approach and the client, but for a wills and probate interview we would recommend advising on the client's matters in this logical order:

- whether any will is valid
- whether the executors are able to act
- the situation relating to any property
- any individual bequests
- the inheritance tax situation
- any potential claims under the estate
- any specific issues that the client wants to raise.

This list emphasises that there are many different points on which the client might need advice. Some issues can be addressed quite quickly, such as advising the client that a bequest is or is not valid. For other points you will need to offer the client a range of options.

## HAVE A GO

Read through the following examples of a candidate applying the law to the facts of the case in **Example 1: wills and probate**. Which do you think is the most successful?

**A** In the case of your father, he did not leave a will. Therefore his estate must be dealt with by way of administration. This means that two people must be appointed to administer the estate, and you will need to decide whether this is something you, and potentially your sister, would be comfortable doing. Once these appointments have been made, the duty of the administrators is to gather in all of the assets of the estate and deal with any liabilities that are owed by the estate. Based on what you have told me, the main asset is the property, and there are few liabilities. It is likely therefore that there will be a substantial amount left after all liabilities have been paid, but because that total value will be below £325,000, it is unlikely that inheritance tax will need to be paid.

The starting point is that you and your sister would be entitled to divide the amount left over between the two of you. However, Angela may have a claim against the estate because she was living with Simon for more than two years. This is because, from what you have told me, she was financially dependent on Simon and may therefore have expected to be provided for in the event of his death. Angela has six months to make a claim from the date that letters of administration are granted, and, if she does so, the administrators will have to decide whether to defend the claim in court proceedings or to attempt to negotiate with her.

**B** In the case of your father, he did not leave a will, which makes things a lot more difficult to deal with. Administrators will need to look after everything and these must be appointed. At the moment you have given me some information but it is not really enough to be able to give proper advice, so I will need to go away and investigate everything more fully; at that point, I can let you know how much inheritance tax will need to be paid. Angela makes things more complicated: she could sue the estate because she was dependent on Simon and if so the court could award her anything, including all of the assets that are in the estate. Therefore, we can't really do anything until we know what the situation is with her.

## COMMENTARY

Example A is a strong example of legal advice. It is clear and structured so that the client can easily follow it from start to finish. It is also respectful and sets out a solid answer based on the information already known, whilst also informing the client that more information will be needed to be completely accurate.

Example B is much weaker. It implicitly criticises the deceased for not making a will, and is overly broad in the analysis of the case, as well as being inaccurate at times. The client is unlikely to leave the office feeling that they are better informed than when they arrived.

## ■ CONCLUDE THE INTERVIEW

We explored how to conclude the interview in Chapter 3, described there as stage 4 of your SQE2 assessment client interview. With a wills and probate interview, it is important to reiterate your sympathy to the client for their loss, and also emphasise the relevance of time limits. If the client is considering making a claim for additional provisions under the Inheritance (Provision for Family and Dependants) Act 1975, time limits will be particularly significant because they must make a claim within six months of probate being granted.

> **Interview technique**
>
> In a wills and probate interview, always ask whether probate has been granted. If it has, the clock will be running for claims against the estate, and you need to work out the relevant dates for enacting your advice. You should include a clear timeframe for future contact with the client when you write the subsequent attendance note.

In any conclusion to an interview, it is crucial to underscore for the client:

- the professional relationship
- the next steps for the client
- the next steps for you.

## HAVE A GO

See below for two different ways of concluding the interview in **Example 1: wills and probate**. Which of these responses is the most appropriate, and would achieve **AC 5** for developing the professional relationship?

A | Well, that's everything. It's been great to see you and we will get on with things for you. I'll send you a letter which summarises everything and we can take it from there. Thanks for coming in.

B | James, I have set out your legal position in respect of all of the points that you have raised, and provided you with some options. Did you understand everything, and do you have any questions? [...]

If anything does occur to you after this meeting, please do get in touch. We will be sending out a client care letter which will set out details of what we have discussed and the fees that will be charged for any future meetings. Our contact details will be on that letter.

Before we finish, it's important to remember that anyone who wishes to make a claim out of the estate has to do so within six months of the letters of appointment being granted, as I explained earlier. Do you have any questions about any of this? [...]

Thank you for coming to see me today. I imagine it must have been difficult in the circumstances and, again, I am very sorry for your loss.

## COMMENTARY

Apart from being too abrupt, Example A is weak on many levels.

- By saying 'that's everything', the candidate leaves the client out of the process. Although you might feel that all the issues have been addressed, the client might disagree. It is therefore important to provide an opportunity for the client to raise any final concerns so that they feel included as the interview draws to a close.
- Saying that it has been 'great' to see the client sets an inappropriate tone for the conclusion to any interview, and particularly one dealing with probate: the reason for the client coming to see you was the loss of a family member. Even if you were appropriately empathic in the beginning of the interview, failing to follow through with a sympathetic tone can negatively impact the relationship with the client.
- 'We will get on with things for you' brings no clarity as to what the solicitor's next steps are. Even if you have already explained this in the interview, you need to reiterate the next stage for the client to ensure that they fully understand.

By contrast, Example B concludes with more depth, is far more empathic to the client and provides clear signposting for them to understand what will be happening next. This kind of response would give the client confidence in your ability to handle the case and would demonstrate competency under **AC 5** for the client interview.

## ■ SUMMARY AND REFLECTION

We hope that these examples have provided some guidance on best practice for the SQE2 client interview assessment and given you confidence to develop your skills further. For this assessment, your approach should be shaped by focusing on the client – the help that they require and the best advice you can provide for them.

Do remember the assessment criteria for client interviewing, included again at the beginning of this chapter. Whilst we have explained the importance of each criterion throughout this book, just rereading them can emphasise the underlying themes: clarity, compassion, confidence and, fundamentally, the client.

# 7

# Practice assessment: wills and probate client interview

This chapter contains a sample client interview in wills and probate for you to attempt. It is a simulation of what happens on the day of the SQE2 assessment, and gives you an opportunity to apply all of the advice provided in the book.

Remember the timings of the assessment:

• Preparation time (reading the email and documents, and making notes): 10 minutes.
• Conducting the interview: 25 minutes.
• Writing the attendance note/legal analysis: 25 minutes.

Make sure that you stick to these times, to replicate the SQE2 assessment as closely as possible.

A client brief is included on page 93 so that a friend or peer can play the role of interviewee. All details in the scenario, including the names and addresses, are fictional.

The accompanying video contains a sample response to this question, with a reflection on the interviewer's performance. A full transcript of the video interview and reflection is given below, and you can see the video at **https://revise4law.co.uk/sqe2-interviewing-video/**.

## ■ QUESTION

### Email to candidate

**From:** Partner
**Sent:** 10 January 202#
**To:** Candidate
**Subject:** Joe Smith (Robyn Smith deceased)

I have received a telephone call from Joe Smith whose husband Robyn died recently following a short illness.

Joe and Robyn had been married for nine years and had no children.

Joe has a copy of Robyn's will (please see copy will of Robyn Smith (Attachment 1)), and wishes to discuss his estate with someone in the firm's probate department.

I have opened a file for her and advised her that you will be dealing with the matter. I have made an appointment for her to see you later today.

Please draft an attendance note of your meeting with Joe for the file.

Thanks

*Ravinder Singh*

**Attachment 1**

LAST WILL AND TESTAMENT OF ROBYN SMITH

I ROBYN SMITH of 12, Devon View, Swansea, SA6 7TT revoke all former wills and testamentary dispositions made by me and declare this to be my last will and testament made on 23rd January 2017.

1    I APPOINT my children Daniel Turner and Katie Turner to be the executors of this Will.
2    I GIVE my sister HANNAH LOWE my emerald ring.
3    I GIVE a legacy of £1,000 to the Dogs Trust.
4    I GIVE the remainder of my estate both real and personal after payment of my funeral and testamentary expenses and any legacy given by this Will and any tax arising in respect of my death to be shared equally between my children Daniel Turner and Katie Turner.

SIGNED BY THE ABOVE NAMED TESTATOR in our joint presence and then by us in theirs.

---

**SIGNED**              *Robyn Smith*

**WITNESSED**

Lewis Reed
3, Sea Close
Swansea
SA2 3KL              *Lewis Reed*
Harry Carter
11, Dylan Vale
Swansea
SA2 3NM              *Harry Carter*

\* \* \*

# ■ YOUR TURN

Have a go at this sample client interview assessment.

## PREPARATION

First, spend ten minutes (1) reading the email to candidate and attached will and (2) making notes, to simulate the SQE2 assessment.

• Think about the legal points raised by this scenario, and try to anticipate your client's needs and objectives.
• Make some notes of points you will want to raise in the interview and further information that you require from the client.
• Try to sketch a plan for the interview so that it flows in a logical and coherent manner.

Hand the client brief on page 93 to a peer, friend or family member and ask them to use it to play the part of the interviewee, Joe Smith. The brief contains some details about the scenario already provided in the email on page 90, but also other information that you as interviewer should discover through carefully questioning the client. It is very important therefore that you **do not read the client brief** before the interview begins.

Refer to Chapter 1 to revise techniques and skills for this part of the SQE2 assessment.

## THE INTERVIEW

When ten minutes have passed, begin the interview. Remember that the SQE2 assessment allows 25 minutes for this, so use the time wisely.

Try to record the interview, so that you can watch it back and assess your performance. A video would be ideal to help you evaluate your body language and eye contact, but an audio recording would also help you to reflect on your performance. If you are unable to record the interview, ask a third person to sit in the practice interview and mark your performance against the assessment criteria.

During the interview, remember to demonstrate all aspects of the assessment criteria for client interviewing:

---

**SQE2 client interviewing assessment criteria**

**Skills**

1. Listen to the client and use questioning effectively to enable the client to tell the solicitor what is important to them.
2. Communicate and explain in a way that is suitable for the client to understand.
3. Conduct themselves in a professional manner and treat the client with courtesy, respect and politeness including respecting diversity where relevant.
4. Demonstrate client-focus in their approach to the client and the issues (ie demonstrate an understanding of the problem from the client's point of view and what the client wants to achieve, not just from a legal perspective).
5. Establish and maintain an effective relationship with the client so as to build trust and confidence.

---

Refer to Chapters 2 and 3 if you need to revise how to meet these assessment criteria.

## THE ATTENDANCE NOTE/LEGAL ANALYSIS

When the interview concludes, you have a further 25 minutes to produce a handwritten attendance note/legal analysis.

Remember that different assessment criteria apply for this component of the SQE2 assessment, and you must demonstrate the following to prove your competency:

---

**SQE2 attendance note/legal analysis assessment criteria**

**Skills**

1. Record all relevant information.
2. Identify appropriate next steps.
3. Provide client-focused advice (ie advice which demonstrates an understanding of the problem from the client's point of view and what the client wants to achieve, not just from a legal perspective).

**Application of law**

4. Apply the law correctly to the client's situation.
5. Apply the law comprehensively to the client's situation, identifying any ethical and professional conduct issues and exercising judgement to resolve them honestly and with integrity.

---

Refer to Chapter 4 if you need to revise your approach to this part of the assessment.

## Client brief

Give this information to the person acting as the client in this assessment, so that they understand the context of the interview and can ask pertinent questions. As interviewer, **DO NOT READ THIS BRIEF** before conducting your interview.

You are Joe Smith, and you are employed as a financial adviser. Your husband, Robyn Smith, died recently and you have a copy of his will (see page 91).

At the time of his death Robyn was employed as a midwife.

Robyn died suddenly following a short illness. You are worried because a month before he died, he told you that he was going to make a new will. However, he did not do this.

You and Robyn were married for nine years and had no children. However, Robyn had two children from a previous relationship: Daniel, who died four years ago aged 24, and Katie, who is a 22-year-old student.

The home that you lived in with Robyn is in your and Robyn's joint names. You believe the property is worth about £300,000.

You have not spoken to Katie (Robyn's daughter) since an argument two years ago. You know that the firm acted for her when she was got into trouble as a teenager, and you would like her address so that you can contact her regarding the will.

**Only raise the following if you are given an opportunity to do so, or are asked appropriate questions:**

- Daniel had a daughter, Phoebe (who is now aged six years).
- The house is owned by you and Robyn as joint tenants in equity.
- Robyn's employers have contacted you, suggesting that you might be entitled to a lump sum under his occupational pension scheme.

Robyn's assets are as follows:
| | |
|---|---|
| Bank account held jointly with you | £8,000 |
| Building society account | £5,000 |
| Shares | £15,000 |

Robyn's liabilities:
| | |
|---|---|
| Funeral expenses | £4,000 |
| Unpaid council tax bill | £750 |

As the client, you particularly want to know:

- As Daniel has died, will Katie be able to act as sole executor of Robyn's estate?
- Robyn's will leaves his 'Emerald ring to his sister Hannah Lowe'. However, you know that Robyn has sold the ring. Will Hannah be entitled to anything from the estate?
- What will happen to Daniel's share of the estate?
- Robyn was helping to pay fees for his elderly mother's nursing home. Will the estate have to continue to provide for this?
- You know that Robyn made a gift of £125,000 to Katie two years ago as a deposit on a flat she was buying. Will this be counted as part of Robyn's estate for inheritance tax purposes?

## EVALUATING YOUR ANSWER

When you have completed the interview and written the attendance note/legal analysis, watch the recording you made and review your attendance note: try to mark your attempt against both SQE2 assessment criteria. Do you think you met the threshold for competency?

Now compare your attempt to the example provided on the accompanying video at **https://revise4law.co.uk/sqe2-interviewing-video/**, for which a full transcript appears below.

The reflection that follows the video (see page 106) gives an evaluation of the client interviewer's attempt, explaining how it demonstrated each part of the assessment criteria and why on balance it would reach the SQE2's threshold standard. Please note, however, that this is not held to be a perfect interview, and the reflection shows where the interviewer's performance could be improved. See if you can spot instances of good practice in the video, and think about how you could reproduce these in your own SQE2 client interview assessment.

A sample attendance note is provided on page 108; compare your attempt with it, and read the commentary provided on how the note manages to demonstrate all aspects of the assessment criteria.

## ■ VIDEO TRANSCRIPT

### GENERAL INTRODUCTION

Hello, my name is Matthew Parry. I'm a lecturer at Swansea Law School, and along with my colleague Amanda Rees I am one of the co-authors of the Revise SQE book on client interviewing and negotiation. These videos are intended to complement the book by giving an example of how an interview might look in the assessment. Before we go into the video, I just want to introduce very briefly who you're going to see on camera. I will be conducting both interviews, the one on property practice and the one on wills and estates. And the client is being played in both cases by Hayley Doyle. And in both cases, obviously, she is playing the fictional client.

In terms of the interviews that you're about to see, we've attempted to make them as close as possible to the exam environment that you will have. There are a couple of small differences:

- In the assessment you are provided with writing materials by the examining body.
- You are not allowed to have a phone in the interview with you because there are clocks in the room. There is a phone on the table in these interviews. That's because I was using it to keep an eye on time. You will not be allowed to have that in the interview itself.

Beyond that, it was as you would expect in the actual assessment. You receive the memo ten minutes before the interview begins and then you have a period of 25 minutes to interview the client. I tried to keep to that; how well I succeed at that, you'll see during the interviews, and I will be doing a reflection on both interviews to summarise my perspective on them and linking what I did to the assessment criteria.

It's important to bear in mind that these are not being held out as perfect interviews. No such thing exists as a perfect interview, but it is an interview that hopefully is one that you will see demonstrating some of the techniques, the skills and the goals that I talk about with Amanda in the book. And I will talk in the reflections a little bit about why I believe these would achieve a pass mark in an assessment.

So enjoy the videos. I hope that you enjoy the book and I hope that you all gain from both the book and the videos when it comes to your assessments. Thank you for watching.

## Preparation

This is the introduction to the wills and probate interview and I'm briefly going to be talking about the materials that I have been provided with ten minutes before my interview. And it's not going to be exact but the idea is that this will replicate, to a degree, the experiences that *you* will have.

So what have I been provided with? Having done all the preparation and anticipated what might happen, the day is finally here. I have the information. What I've been provided with is a memo to trainee and the last will and testament of Robyn Smith.

Looking at the memo to begin with, I know that my client's name is Joe Smith and I know that her husband has died recently following a short illness.

One thing to note is that the names are likely, as in this case, to be gender-neutral, so you may not know whether you will be interviewing Mr Joe Smith or Mrs Joe Smith, but that doesn't matter. Don't worry too much about that. Obviously, you can adapt when you see your client [*and check the pronouns that they would prefer to use*].

Obviously, we know that Robyn has died, so immediately I'm going to make a note to remind myself to be sympathetic and to express my condolences when I first see the client.

Looking at the relevant points from the memo, I can see that they have had no children. They've been married for nine years. Nothing particularly flags up from that. There is a copy of the will and they wish to discuss the estate with someone in the firm's probate department. So there isn't a huge amount there.

But, turning to the will itself, there are some additional points that are noteworthy:

- We can see that Robyn has appointed his children, Daniel and Katie, to be executors. Now, that conflicts with the memo information that they had no children, which implies that Robyn has children from another relationship. Obviously, I'm going to want to ask questions about them.
- Specific legacies to Hannah: an emerald ring. I'm going to want to ask about that, to see what the status of the ring is.
- There's a legacy to the Dogs Trust: that will have implications for inheritance tax.
- And then, finally, the estate is given to Daniel and Katie. What is noteworthy here is that there's no mention of Joe Smith in the will. So that is something that I'm going to explore:
  - It may be that there is property, so that is the effective bequest to Joe.
  - It may be that Joe will want to look at bringing proceedings to gain a greater share out of the estate.

These are all questions that now have flagged up in my mind, as well as the general information I'm going to want to ask about financial details, etc. And that is effectively what I'm now going to solidify: I've probably spent three or four minutes calculating that. I've now got another five or six minutes to jot down a few things and begin to work on how I'm going to approach the interview.

So that is the information that I can gather from the memo to trainee and the last will and testament of Robyn Smith that I have received ten minutes before the interview itself.

## THE INTERVIEW

**Candidate:** Hello, is it Joe Smith?

**Client:**    Yes, that's right.

**Candidate:** Hello, my name's Matthew Parry. I'm a trainee solicitor at this firm and I'll be speaking to you today about the matter that you've come in to see us about. Did you manage to find us OK?

**Client:**    Yes, that was all right.

**Candidate:** Did you drive here?

**Client:**    Yes.

**Candidate:** I hope you didn't have any issues with parking.

**Client:**    No, thankfully. I found a spot right away, so that worked out OK.

**Candidate:** OK, good. First and foremost, I understand that you're here to see us about your late husband, Robyn Smith. Is that correct?

**Client:**    Yes. That's right.

**Candidate:** Well, please accept my sympathies on your loss. I imagine it's been a difficult time for you. How long were you married for?

**Client:**    For nine years.

**Candidate:** Nine years? I imagine it's been a difficult time. Please do take your time throughout this process. If you have any questions, if you need a pause, a break, please don't hesitate, OK? This is very much your time, your space, and don't hesitate to ask if I can help with anything, OK? As I say, I understand that you want to speak to me about Robyn's will, and we will get to that, we'll go through it. Do you have a copy of that will with you?

**Client:**    I do, yes.

**Candidate:** And have you had the chance to read it?

**Client:**    Yes.

**Candidate:** OK. We'll be going through that in some detail. Before we do that, there are a few matters I just need to chat about. Have you been to see a solicitor before?

**Client:**    It's been a while.

**Candidate:** Well, every solicitor's firm deals with things differently anyway, so I'm just going to take you through what the process of the interview is going to be like so that you have some certainty over that. So we've got about 25 minutes for this interview. The main purpose is for me to be able to help you to understand the will, what it means for you, and if there's anything we need to do or you need to do. OK?

In order to get to that point, I'll be asking some detailed information, primarily about Robyn, about yourself and about the financial situation.

Again, some of these details are going to be quite personal, so I apologise in advance, but the more that I understand about the situation, the more it is likely that I'll be able to help you.

So, again, if you're uncertain about why I'm asking anything, don't hesitate to ask. OK? What is really important, particularly in that light, is that everything that you say to me is confidential. And what that means is I can't go and say it to anyone else outside this firm. That means that the more you can help me with, the more I can help you to understand the situation.

There are a couple of exceptions to the confidentiality rules. I don't want you to worry about those. If it looks like we're getting to a point where one may be coming up, I'll stop, I'll explain it to you, and we'll talk about where we want to go from there. But, for now, don't let that worry you, OK?

As I say, I'll be asking a lot of questions. If *you* have any questions at any point, please ask me. As I say, this is your interview, your space, so don't hesitate to ask me. You don't need to wait till the end. Just ask at any point. I'll make sure at the end that you've asked everything that you want before we end the interview. OK?

So if I can just ask a few questions, on a personal nature; what's your full name?

**Client:**      Joe Smith.

**Candidate:** Joe Smith. And what's your address?

**Client:**      12 Devon View, Swansea.

**Candidate:** OK. I can see that that was the address in the will, so was that the address that you shared with Robyn?

**Client:**      Yes, that's right.

**Candidate:** OK. And did you have – you've been married for nine years, you said –

**Client:**      That's right.

**Candidate:** Did you have any children together?

**Client:**      No.

**Candidate:** No, OK. Did you or Robyn, or *do* you or Robyn have any other children?

**Client:**      Robyn had two from a previous relationship: Katie and Daniel.

**Candidate:** Katie and Daniel. So how old are Katie and Daniel?

**Client:**      Katie's 22. She's a student, and Daniel unfortunately passed away four years ago, and he was 24.

**Candidate:** I'm very sorry. That must have been a horrendous loss.

**Client:**      Yes, definitely.

**Candidate:** I'm very sorry. And that was four years ago?

**Client:** Yes. That's right.

**Candidate:** OK. Did Daniel or does Katie have any children?

**Client:** Daniel has a daughter who's six now.

**Candidate:** OK. And his/her name?

**Client:** Phoebe.

**Candidate:** Phoebe. Thank you. OK. Where did Robyn work?

**Client:** He was a midwife.

**Candidate:** Midwife? He was a midwife. And do you work?

**Client:** Yes, I'm a financial adviser.

**Candidate:** A financial adviser. So very different jobs!

**Client:** Yes.

**Candidate:** All right. So what I'm going to ask you now is a bit about the financial situation. And this is effectively to get an idea as to Robyn's estate, and this is important so that we can understand and advise on potential tax implications later. Again, we don't need the exact details, but just a broad figure, if you have it, would be helpful. We can always look at this in more detail later. So, again, we're just trying to get a broad picture at the moment.

**Client:** Right.

**Candidate:** Do you own 12 Devon View together? You live[d] there together; is it a jointly owned property?

**Client:** Yes. Both of our names are on the property.

**Candidate:** OK. And when you purchased the property, do you recall what the solicitor said about how you owned it together?

**Client:** I think he said it was joint tenants in equity.

**Candidate:** OK, so joint tenants in equity. Don't worry if you're not 100% sure, because we can check that. It's a very easy thing to check. OK. And did Robyn have any bank accounts, either that he had individually or that are joint with you?

**Client:** Yes, we had a joint bank account and then [he had] a building society account as well.

**Candidate:** OK. So the joint account, because it was in both your names, that now becomes *your* account. The single account, his own building society account – how much was approximately in it, do you know?

**Client:**   I think £5,000.

**Candidate:**   £5,000. OK. Do you know if he had any shares or stocks?

**Client:**   Yes, shares for sure.

**Candidate:**   OK. Any idea about the approximate value?

**Client:**   Close to £15,000, I think.

**Candidate:**   £15,000. And do you know if he had any insurance or pension plans?

**Client:**   I have been contacted about a pension plan, yes.

**Candidate:**   OK. Who contacted you?

**Client:**   His employers contacted me.

**Candidate:**   So, his employers, it was potentially an employment plan that he signed up to.

**Client:**   Yes.

**Candidate:**   OK. Did they say if they were contacting you because of any particular reason?

**Client:**   Yes. They said I might be entitled to a lump sum under the scheme.

**Candidate:**   So that suggests that you were a nominated person on that account, which means effectively that that money would go directly to you irrespective of what the will says.

**Client:**   OK.

**Candidate:**   Any idea about how much that is, approximately?

**Client:**   No idea, no.

**Candidate:**   Again, that's something we can look into. This is perhaps too broad a question, but do you know if Robyn had any particularly valuable items – art, antiques, jewellery – anything along those lines?

**Client:**   Not that I can think of. The only thing would be the emerald ring in the will.

**Candidate:**   The one named in the will.

**Client:**   Yes, but I do have some other questions about that, once we get to the will.

**Candidate:**   OK, well, we can cover that when we get to it, and we'll cross that bridge at that point, which is in a few minutes.

**Client:**   Perfect.

**Candidate:**   So how much is the property worth, approximately, 12 Devon View?

**Client:**   I think £300,000.

**Candidate:** £300,000. And do you know if Robyn gave any gifts to anyone in the last seven years? When I say gifts, I mean significant gifts: more than £3,000.

**Client:** Yes. About two years ago, he gave Katie a gift. It was about putting a deposit on the flat that she was buying at the time, and that was about £125,000.

**Candidate:** OK, now that's helpful. The reason I'm asking these questions is so we can potentially look if there is likely to be any inheritance tax liability. And that does help with that; I will give you some advice on that later.

**Client:** That would be great.

**Candidate:** Now, in terms of the will itself, did you say you had some questions about this?

**Client:** Yes.

**Candidate:** OK. Well, before we get to those questions, the first and the most important thing is, it does appear, on the face of it, to be a valid will. And what I mean by that is it is signed by Robyn and it has two witnesses who do not appear to be connected to him. Now that means that this is the valid will or *a* valid will, and this will set out what will happen to his estate.

**Client:** OK. Now, he had told me that he had wanted to make a new will, but he hadn't done that yet. Does that impact this at all?

**Candidate:** It doesn't impact the validity of this will but there are potential options for you that we can explore later. So I'll make a note of that and we'll come back to that.

**Client:** Perfect.

**Candidate:** And you're quite certain that he didn't get around to writing a new will?

**Client:** Not that I know of, no.

**Candidate:** Right. That's helpful because we will cover that later. But thank you for raising that. In terms of the will, he appoints Daniel and Katie, so his children, to be executors of the will.

**Client:** Yes.

**Candidate:** Now, I'm anticipating that a question you may be asking is about Daniel no longer, unfortunately, being with us; what the situation is.

**Client:** Yes.

**Candidate:** You can have two executors. You can also have one executor. So the will is still valid even with just Katie as an executor.

**Client:** So she'll be the sole executor.

**Candidate:** She will be the sole executor. If she wants to, it's possible to appoint additional executors. But it is possible for there to simply be one executor.

**Client:** OK. I was hoping to get in contact with Katie just about the world generally, and I believe she used this firm ages ago for something; I'm not really sure. So I was hoping I could get her address from you, just so I can write to her and try and get some of this sorted with her.

**Candidate:** OK. I can fully understand why you'd be asking for that information. It's important that you do communicate with each other. Unfortunately, I can't confirm whether Katie is or has ever been a client of this firm. You remember at the start we talked about client confidentiality. In the same way that I owe you a duty of confidentiality, I owe that same duty to every other client. So I don't know if Katie was a client to this firm. That's something I can check but I wouldn't be able to tell you whether she was or not. Nor could I hand out her information if she was. I do appreciate why you were asking but, unfortunately, that's something I can't do.

The best thing I could do here, if you were willing, if you were happy for me to pass your contact information on to Katie, if it turns out she is a member, a client of the firm, then I can do that if you authorised me to do that.

**Client:** Yes, that actually would be really great.

**Candidate:** OK. If you could drop me an email, simply confirming that you're instructing me to do that, then I will be able to check. And if it turns out that Katie has been a member, a client of this firm, I will then be able to pass your information on to her once you've officially instructed me to do so.

**Candidate:** OK, perfect.

**Candidate:** I'm sorry I can't be more help there.

**Client:** That's – I understand.

**Candidate:** Katie will be able to be the executor. If Katie were to not want to be an executor, then effectively there'd have to be new executors appointed or an administrator of the estate. But, again, that's a bridge we can cross if necessary, when we come to it. And, again, finding out whether Katie wants to be an executor is the first and most important point there. Now, moving down, the next point is that Robyn gives his sister Hannah an emerald ring. Is Hannah still alive?

**Client:** Yes.

**Candidate:** She is, OK. You said you had a question about the ring.

**Client:** Yes, I know that he sold the ring a while ago, maybe eight months ago. So [I'm] just wondering, then, what Hannah is entitled to, given that the ring has been sold.

**Candidate:** OK, so to be clear, he sold the ring before he passed away?

**Client:** That's right. Yes.

**Candidate:** OK. The simple answer, unfortunately for Hannah, is that she's not entitled to anything because it was a specific gift. That specific gift no longer exists. Therefore, it is deemed to be – deemed, that's the legal phrase – [that] she is not entitled to anything. [For] some gifts, the estate will have to pay the equivalent. So, for example, if he said that 'I give my sister Hannah Lowe 500 BT shares', the estate would have to buy 500 BT shares. That's not in here. So, that gift effectively simply fails. And again, unfortunately for Hannah, she's not entitled to anything.

**Client:**    OK.

**Candidate:**    The next is a legacy of £1,000 to the Dogs Trust. Dogs Trust is a charity that is still in existence, so the estate would have to pay that money to the Dogs Trust. That £1,000, however, would not be used for any calculation of inheritance tax because it's a charity.

**Client:**    Right.

**Candidate:**    And then the remainder goes to Daniel and Katie. Now, Katie is not an issue because I think you said she was 22.

**Client:**    Yes, that's right.

**Candidate:**    So Katie's half is not a problem. In respect of Daniel, there isn't a substitution clause in the will to say that, if one of these people passes away, this person replaces them. However, because Daniel has a daughter, Phoebe, his share will automatically go to her.

**Client:**    Right.

**Candidate:**    She is, I think you said, six? Four, sorry. I apologise, how old did you say? Six?

**Client:**    Six.

**Candidate:**    She is six. So, because of that, the money would be held on trust for her until she turns 18, but that's not something you have to worry about. That's something for the estate to worry about – or Katie, effectively.

**Client:**    OK.

**Candidate:**    And that essentially is the end of the will. Now, that does not leave anything to you.

**Client:**    Right.

**Candidate:**    That being said, you said that the property, which is not mentioned in the will, you believed it was held as joint tenants.

**Client:**    Yes, I'm pretty sure it is.

**Candidate:**    So, in terms of the property, if that is correct, that property will be transferred from your joint names to your sole name; you will own that property. If it is held as tenants in common – and we can check this, but your memory is it was held as joint tenancy – if it were the other way, then his share would fall as part of the will to, effectively, Phoebe and Katie.

**Client:**    Right.

**Candidate:** So it's important that we check that. But, based on what you've said, the property will be yours. So, even though you're not named in the will, you will still get the property.

**Client:** Perfect.

**Candidate:** And that's something we'll talk about later, about how we can check that.

**Client:** OK.

**Candidate:** Now, in terms of the will, because you're not mentioned, do you feel – and particularly you said that you were told he was doing a new will – do you feel that you should have been entitled to something else under the will, or is there anyone else who you feel might take that view?

**Client:** I can't think of anything for myself. The only thing is that he was helping to pay his mother's nursing home fees. So would the estate still have to pay for that, then?

**Candidate:** So his mother is in a care home?

**Client:** A nursing home, that's right.

**Candidate:** And Robyn was paying for the nursing home fees?

**Client:** Yes. I'm not sure if it was all of them or just part of them, but was making contributions, anyway.

**Candidate:** Under the will, the answer is no, because they're not mentioned. There is provision for anyone who feels that they should have been provided for under the will to make a claim to the courts within six months of probate being granted. They effectively are saying to the courts: I was dependent upon this person; I should have been provided for.

**Client:** OK.

**Candidate:** So Robyn's mother could technically do that. She could make an application. That doesn't mean she would get anything. It would not affect your property. It would only affect the amounts that are in the estate and would go to Katie and Phoebe. But if Robyn's mother would wish to do that, or if you were to decide you would want to do that, then you could. You would just have to make the decision within six months of the grant of probate.

**Client:** OK. And then I would do that, if I wanted to make an application, I would do that through where?

**Candidate:** It's through the court. So effectively you can instruct us to do it or another set of lawyers, another set of solicitors. Or you could do it yourself. You apply to the court. You have to demonstrate that you have been supported and maintained, or provided for, by Robyn. Then the court makes a decision as to whether an appropriate amount should be paid.

**Client:** OK.

**Candidate:**   And that's something we can advise you on in more detail if you do wish to consider going down that route. Do you know if probate has been granted on this?

**Client:**   I don't know.

**Candidate:**   Well, if it has, the clock will have started running because it's six months. If not, then, it starts to run in terms of six months from the time that probate is granted.

**Client:**   OK.

**Candidate:**   OK? So that deals with that particular point. Were there any other questions that you had?

**Client:**   I don't think so. I think – did we talk about the inheritance tax with the £125,000 [gift to Katie]?

**Candidate:**   So, in terms of that, the way that inheritance tax works is: inheritance tax applies if the estate is worth more than £325,000. Now, I've done obviously a very quick calculation – this would be something for the executor's solicitors to do – but the property doesn't affect the situation significantly because it's a joint tenancy. So it's not part of the estate, it's outside the estate. But even if – how much is the property worth, approximately?

**Client:**   £300,000.

**Candidate:**   Even if a nominal valuation of £150,000 would be taken for his share, £5,000, you said in a bank account, £15,000 in shares, the only significant thing here is the gift to Katie. Now, because that was less than seven years ago, that would still be counted for inheritance tax purposes. But, even with that added in, it still does not come up to £325,000.

**Client:**   Right.

**Candidate:**   It doesn't look – although it is relevant for inheritance tax purposes, it doesn't look like it's going to seriously affect it. And, again, the property is outside the estate, so that would not be affected.

**Client:**   OK.

**Candidate:**   OK? Do you have any other questions that I can help you with?

**Client:**   No, I don't. I think that's everything.

**Candidate:**   OK. Well, I'm just going to very quickly summarise. You obviously have come to see me because of the sad passing of your late husband. We've gone through the will together and explored the various points from it, in particular the unfortunate death of Daniel and how that affects the executors, and that his share will go to his daughter when she reaches 18.

Hannah is not entitled to anything from the will because the emerald ring has been sold, and the executors will deal with everything in respect to this, which is now just Katie, including any potential claims from Robyn['s mother]. If you want to bring a claim, because you feel that you should have been provided for, you have to do so within six months effectively from probate being granted.

The only step that I really would advise going forward is that we make sure of the situation with the house. The easiest way to do that: we can pull up the Land Registry documents, assuming it's registered, and that will tell us whether it's joint tenants or tenants in common. And, again, we will explain how much that will cost in our client care letter that will follow.

**Client:**    Perfect.

**Candidate:** Does that all make sense to you?

**Client:**    Yes. And I'll just email you then about getting my details to Katie?

**Candidate:** Absolutely. If you email me authority to do that – literally 'I authorise you to do that' – then I can get on with that. I can at least check to see if Katie has ever been a client of this firm.

**Client:**    Perfect, that's great.

**Candidate:** OK. Now, in terms of what happens next: from your perspective, you need to email me that; from our perspective, we'll send out a full client care letter explaining what's happened today, explaining our fees if you want us to go forward, including any specific action like determining if it is a joint tenancy or not. What is the best way of getting that to you?

**Client:**    Probably email is best.

**Candidate:** What's the best email address for you?

**Client:**    Yes, just Joe dot Smith.

**Candidate:** Is that J-O-E?

**Client:**    That's right. Dot Smith at hotmail.com.

**Candidate:** Thank you very much. And just so I have it on file, what's the best telephone number for you?

**Client:**    07647 512412.

**Candidate:** Thank you. I will still send a hard copy to 12 Devon View, if that's OK, just to make sure that you have a copy there, but we will also email a copy to you so that you've got that as quickly as possible. If you have any questions, our contact details will be in there. There is also a section that deals with who you can speak to at the firm if you have any concerns that you would like to raise, and also some alternative people you'll be able to speak to if I'm unavailable for any reason. But, apart from that, do you have any questions that I can help you with?

**Client:**    No, I think I'm set.

**Candidate:** OK, well, please, once again, accept my condolences on the loss of Robyn. Thank you very much for making the time to come and see us today, and please do not hesitate to get in touch if I can assist with anything further.

**Client:**    Thanks so much.

**Candidate:** Thank you.

## REFLECTION

This is my reflection on the wills and estates interview that I have just conducted with the client, Joe Smith, played ably by Hayley.

I'm going to break the reflection into two parts. The first part of the reflection will be my personal thoughts on it and where it could have been improved. The second will be with reference to the assessment criteria that you can find under assessments in SQE2, online or in any preparatory materials that you have. [*See page 92 for the assessment criteria.*]

So how did the interview go? And a reminder: this is *not* held out as a perfect interview. There is no such thing. Every interview can be improved. No interview will ever be a complete write-off or a complete success. What I think did go well in that interview was, I believe, that I developed a bond with the client, a professional bond that was based on empathy and awareness of her particular situation.

I didn't go over the top but I gave the client the space to express their concerns and the time and awareness of that time to be able to ask questions. I gathered the details that I needed and I was able to advise on all the relevant points without confusing the client or going into unnecessary detail.

Because the client is not an executor in this situation, there were some points I could have gone into further but did not need to. Inheritance tax is relevant but not crucial to this client. If I were representing someone who was going to be an executor, that would be far more of a situation that I'd need to consider.

Likewise, the client said that she did not want to pursue a claim against the estate. There was nothing to indicate that that would be a strong claim. I could have gone into that in more detail but, again, it didn't seem necessary to do so.

So the advice was fairly clear. The crucial point from her perspective was the property, because that was going to be her sole legacy under the estate.

Where the interview could have been improved: I've already talked a little about going into more detail on a potential claim that she might have. I certainly had a couple of minutes spare that I could have done that with, but also I could have got some more detail about the liabilities under the estate. I went into detail about the assets but, once it was clear that inheritance tax was unlikely to apply, I didn't pursue the liabilities. That I certainly could and should have done, in order to maximise the information that I had. Ideally, you want to be in a situation where you're not asking additional information in a subsequent correspondence.

So there are some things I could have improved. But overall and looking at the assessment criteria, looking at the skills:

1.  Listen to the client and use questioning effectively to enable the client to tell the solicitor what is important to them.

    Did I listen to the client and use questioning effectively to enable the client to tell the solicitor what is important to them? Yes. I could have asked the question more clearly, 'what is of most importance to you?' but, without even without that question, the broad point did come across.
2.  Communicate and explain in a way that is suitable for the client to understand.

    I tried to avoid legalese – point 2, communicate and explain in a way that is suitable for the client to understand. Where I did use phrases that were legalistic, I did try to explain them.

3.  Conduct themselves in a professional manner and treat the client with courtesy, respect and politeness including respecting diversity where relevant.

    I believe I conducted myself in a professional manner and treated the client with courtesy, respect and politeness.

4.  Demonstrate client-focus in their approach to the client and the issues (ie demonstrate an understanding of the problem from the client's point of view and what the client wants to achieve, not just from a legal perspective).

    And, again, I demonstrated an understanding of the problem from the client's point of view and what the client wants to achieve, rather than just what the critical legal questions were. Again, there were a few questions that perhaps were more focused around the executor rather than a potential beneficiary, but trying to strike that balance is key, and I believe I did do that.

5.  Establish and maintain an effective relationship with the client so as to build trust and confidence.

    I could have phrased my icebreaking questions a little more specifically but, again, I think those were important to help draw the client out before I expressed condolences.

So, looking at the assessment criteria for an interview, I believe that I hit the marks on those five criteria. I also believe I had sufficient information to be able to write up an attendance note on this, which of course is the second part of your assessment that you move into after you've conducted the interview.

So, overall, although there were areas that could have been improved, I was happy with the way that this interview went.

# ■ SAMPLE ATTENDANCE NOTE/LEGAL ANALYSIS

### Attending Joe Smith regarding late spouse's estate – Robyn Smith

[This attendance note includes all the financial information from the Client brief, even though, as noted in the Reflection on page 106, not all of it was gathered in this interview.]

**Date:**    DD/MM/YY
**Time:**    10.00–10.25
**Client:**    Joe Smith
**Matter:**    Estate of Robyn Smith, deceased

## Deceased
**DOB:** 16 July 1970
**DOD**: TBC from death certificate
Worked as midwife
Will made 23 January 2017. Death was sudden.

## Family
Robyn had two children from a previous relationship

- Daniel (24, now deceased)
- Katie (22, student). Received a gift of £125,000 for a deposit on a house from Robyn two years ago.

Client is not in contact with Katie. Client thinks that the firm acted for Katie in the past and asked us to pass on her contact details to Katie. I explained that this was not possible due to confidentiality.

Daniel has a daughter aged 6.

## Assets and liabilities

### Assets
Joe and Robyn jointly owned the house, 12 Devon View. Client believed that the property was owned as joint tenants.

- Approximate value: £300,000.

Other assets stated to be:

- Joint bank account: £8,000
- Building Society account: £5,000
- Shares: £15,000

Potential for pension scheme payment (work).

## Liabilities

Liabilities stated to be:

- Funeral expenses (£4,000)
- Unpaid bills (£750)

Approximate total of assets = £328,000
Approximate total of liabilities = £4,750

As the property was held as joint tenants (so only half the value is relevant) and Joe is the spouse to Robyn (so the transfer would not qualify for tax), inheritance tax is unlikely to be an issue even if the gift to Katie is included.

## Advice

I advised that the will was valid and that, although Joe was not named in the will, the house was in joint tenancy and so they would be entitled to keep that. Likewise the joint bank account.

Client had a number of questions about the situation. I answered as follows:

Two executors are named, but Daniel has died. Is Katie the sole executor?
- Katie will be able to act as the sole executor as long as she is happy to take on this responsibility.

Emerald ring: this is left to Hannah but the ring was sold before death.
- This is a specific rather than a general gift and therefore it has been adeemed. Hannah not entitled to anything from the estate.

Daniel is a beneficiary under the will. What happens to his estate?
- This would pass to his daughter (Phoebe) but she is a minor so the money would be put into a trust for her. Need to clarify with client that this depends on any will left by Daniel before he died.

Robyn has been paying for his mother's nursing home fees. Is the estate responsible?
- Estate would not be responsible but his mother may have a claim under the Inheritance (Provision for Family and Dependants) Act 1975, based on whether or not she was being partially or fully maintained by Robyn prior to death. Would be decided by the courts, including what, if any, award would be appropriate.

Gift: Robyn gifted £125,000 to Katie two years ago for a deposit.
- This may form part of the estate as it is within the seven-year period for gifts prior to death. It would need to be taken into account for Inheritance Act tax purposes but the figures suggest this will not be payable.

## Next steps for client and firm

1. Write a client care letter to the client to summarise the meeting.
2. Confirm with the Land Registry whether the property is held as joint tenants.
3. Make enquiries about deceased's pension.
4. Ask for written authority to ascertain whether or not Katie is a client and, if so, to write to her and explain the situation about Robyn's will.

## COMMENTARY

On balance, the candidate has met the threshold standard for the attendance note/legal analysis component of the SQE2 client interview assessment:

- **AC 1** Record all relevant information: The candidate has included key facts set out in the assessment documents and elicited in the client interview, in particular the range of concerns that the client has, the details behind them and the advice given.
- **AC 2** Identify appropriate next steps: The candidate has identified that they would write to Joe setting out the advice and next steps, and has included a note that additional instructions will be needed in writing to allow them to contact an existing client.
- **AC 3** Provide client-focused advice: The candidate has demonstrated an understanding of the client's concerns from the client's perspective and has provided appropriate solutions.
- **AC 4** Apply the law correctly: The candidate has identified the relevant fundamental legal principles and applied them correctly to the facts of the client's case. The candidate has identified the crucial tests for an adeemed gift and an awareness of the relevant tax bands of the Inheritance Act.
- **AC 5** Apply the law comprehensively: The candidate's advice is sufficiently detailed in the context of the factual issues. For example, the candidate has explained that they cannot break confidentiality with any existing client, and has explained the consequences of one of the executors having died.

## ■ SUMMARY AND REFLECTION

The nature of interviewing for the wills and probate SQE2 assessment is formulaic. Once you have ascertained whether or not there is a will, you will have a clear idea of the direction that you want to follow, and this should provide you with a certain amount of confidence in your preparation.

However, whilst it is reassuring to be able to identify the inevitable questions that must be asked, for example details of the assets and liabilities, it is also essential that you do not overlook the very personal nature of the interview. The client will almost certainly have very specific questions, and it is important that you give your full attention to what they are asking and why. This interview provided a good example of when you might need to think more about why the client was asking a question: her enquiry about Robyn's mother's potential claim. In the interview the candidate answered the question accurately enough, but he could have gone further in reassuring the client that the court, if necessary, would take her own concerns into account as well, and that in any event the property was outside the will and therefore would not be touched by the court. Keep the assessment criteria and especially **AC 4** in your mind at all times: remain client-focused and view the issue from the client's perspective.

In terms of the attendance note, remember that detail is important. You need to be as precise as you can with the figures, including identifying, where necessary, where there is any uncertainty. You also need to give an accurate record of what was discussed and the advice you gave, including your legal analysis of the case. Remember that the assessment criteria are different from the client interview, and you need to demonstrate your skills and application of law for this part of the assessment.

# 8

# Practice assessment: property client interview

This chapter contains a sample client interview in property for you to attempt. It is a simulation of what happens on the day of the SQE2 assessment and gives you an opportunity to apply all of the advice provided in the book.

Remember the timings of the assessment:

- Preparation time (reading the email and documents, and making notes): 10 minutes.
- Conducting the interview: 25 minutes.
- Writing the attendance note/legal analysis: 25 minutes.

Make sure that you stick to these times, to replicate the SQE2 assessment as closely as possible.

A client brief is included on page 114 so that a friend or peer can play the role of interviewee. All details in the scenario, including the names and addresses, are fictional.

The accompanying video contains a sample response to this question, with a reflection on the interviewer's performance. A full transcript of the video interview and reflection is given below, and you can see a recording of the video at **https://revise4law.co.uk/ sqe2-interviewing-video/**.

## ■ QUESTION

### Email to candidate

**From:** Partner
**Sent:** 10 January 202#
**To:** Candidate
**Subject:** Joe Smith (property matter)

I have received a telephone call from Joe Smith who needs to speak to us about a property matter. S/he wants to sell the property in the future and is unsure about some issues with ownership and boundaries.

Please draft an attendance note of your meeting with Joe for the file.

Thanks

*Ravinder Singh*

\*  \*  \*

# ■ YOUR TURN

Have a go at this sample client interview assessment.

## PREPARATION

First, spend ten minutes reading the email to candidate and making notes, to simulate the SQE2 assessment.

- Although the email is short, think about possible legal points that might arise, and try to anticipate your client's needs and objectives.
- Make some notes of points you will want to raise in the interview and information that you require from the client.
- Try to sketch a plan for the interview so that it flows in a logical and coherent manner.

Hand the client brief on page 114 to a peer, friend or family member and ask them to use it to play the part of the interviewee, Joe Smith. The brief contains some details about the scenario already provided in the email on page 111, but also other information that you as interviewer should discover through carefully questioning the client. It is very important therefore that you **do not read the client brief** before the interview begins.

Look back at Chapter 1 if you need to revise techniques and skills for this part of the SQE2 assessment.

## THE INTERVIEW

When ten minutes have passed, begin the interview. Remember that the SQE2 assessment allows 25 minutes for this, so use the time wisely.

Try to record the interview, so that you can watch it back and assess your performance. A video would be ideal to help you evaluate your body language and eye contact, but an audio recording would also help you to reflect on your performance. If you are unable to record the interview, ask a third person to sit in the practice interview and mark your performance against the assessment criteria.

During the interview, remember to demonstrate all aspects of the assessment criteria for client interviewing:

---

### SQE2 client interviewing assessment criteria

#### Skills

1. Listen to the client and use questioning effectively to enable the client to tell the solicitor what is important to them.
2. Communicate and explain in a way that is suitable for the client to understand.
3. Conduct themselves in a professional manner and treat the client with courtesy, respect and politeness including respecting diversity where relevant.
4. Demonstrate client-focus in their approach to the client and the issues (ie demonstrate an understanding of the problem from the client's point of view and what the client wants to achieve, not just from a legal perspective).
5. Establish and maintain an effective relationship with the client so as to build trust and confidence.

---

Refer to Chapters 2 and 3 if you need to revise how to meet these assessment criteria.

## THE ATTENDANCE NOTE/LEGAL ANALYSIS

When the interview concludes, you have a further 25 minutes to produce a handwritten attendance note/legal analysis.

Remember that different assessment criteria apply for this component of the SQE2 assessment, and you must demonstrate the following to prove your competency:

---

### SQE2 attendance note/legal analysis assessment criteria

#### Skills

1.  Record all relevant information.
2.  Identify appropriate next steps.
3.  Provide client-focused advice (ie advice which demonstrates an understanding of the problem from the client's point of view and what the client wants to achieve, not just from a legal perspective).

#### Application of law

4.  Apply the law correctly to the client's situation.
5.  Apply the law comprehensively to the client's situation, identifying any ethical and professional conduct issues and exercising judgement to resolve them honestly and with integrity.

---

Refer to Chapter 4 if you need to revise your approach to this part of the assessment.

The client brief to hand to the person playing the role of client is included overleaf, but remember **not to read this** before conducting your interview.

## Client brief

Give this information to the person acting as the client in this assessment, so that they understand the context of the interview and can ask pertinent questions. As interviewer, **DO NOT READ THIS BRIEF** before conducting your interview.

You are Joe Smith and own a property: 17 George Close, Swansea SA1 1PP. This is where you live and so this is your contact address. You can make up any other contact details such as email address and telephone number if you are asked for them during the interview.

You want to sell the property in the near future but have a number of questions about the property that you need to address before making the decision to sell.

1.  The main issue is how much money you will be entitled to receive from the property. The value is approximately £300,000 and there is a mortgage of around £250,000. You anticipate legal costs and stamp duty being around £7,500.

    You purchased this property jointly with your father, who has since passed away. The title deeds for the property have not been changed yet, so it remains in both of your names.

    You have a stepsister, Amelia, who received everything from your father's estate when he died. She has recently been in touch to say that she is entitled to half of this property when it sells, and has demanded that you pay her £150,000 after sale. This has scared you very much.

2.  You are also concerned about the fences on both sides of the property. You think that the neighbours to the right own that boundary fence, but they have not maintained it and their dog keeps escaping into your property. On the left, you believe that you own it but you are not sure, and are worried that potential buyers might not like the fence.

**Only raise the following if you are given an opportunity to do so, or are asked appropriate questions:**

*   About three months before he died, your father mentioned putting your rights over the property into some form of agreed document, with the idea that he would have 10% and you 90%, as he wanted to make sure that your interest in the property was protected. His illness accelerated and this did not progress beyond initial discussions.
*   There is a stone birdbath that is built into the back garden, cemented into the ground. It was carved by your father when he was alive and has great sentimental value to you. Can you take it with you when you sell?
*   You want to move to London when you have sold the house. You would like to stop making mortgage payments to save some money.

As the client, you particularly want to know:

*   What is the legal position regarding the amount of money that you can realise from the sale of the property?
*   What are your responsibilities regarding the fences on either side of the house?
*   What can you do with the stone birdbath?
*   To save money for your move to London, can you stop paying the mortgage now as you know you want to sell the property?

## EVALUATING YOUR ANSWER

When you have completed the interview and written the attendance note/legal analysis, watch the recording you made and review your attendance note: try to mark your attempt against both SQE2 assessment criteria. Do you think you met the threshold for competency?

Now compare your attempt to the example provided on the accompanying video at **https://revise4law.co.uk/sqe2-interviewing-video/**, for which a full transcript appears below.

The reflection which follows the video (see page 129) gives an evaluation of the client interviewer's attempt, explaining how it demonstrated each part of the assessment criteria and why on balance it would reach the SQE2's threshold standard. Please note, however, that this is not held to be a perfect interview, and the reflection shows where the interviewer's performance could be improved. See if you can spot instances of good practice in the video and think about how you could reproduce these in your own SQE2 client interview assessment.

A sample attendance note is provided on page 131; compare your attempt with it, and read the commentary provided on how the note manages to demonstrate all aspects of the assessment criteria.

## ◼ VIDEO TRANSCRIPT

## GENERAL INTRODUCTION

Hello, my name is Matthew Parry. I'm a lecturer at Swansea Law School, and along with my colleague Amanda Rees I am one of the co-authors of the Revise SQE book on client interviewing and negotiation. These videos are intended to complement the book by giving an example of how an interview might look in the assessment. Before we go into the video, I just want to introduce very briefly who you're going to see on camera. I will be conducting both interviews, the one on property practice and the one on wills and estates. And the client is being played in both cases by Hayley Doyle. And in both cases, obviously, she is playing the fictional client.

In terms of the interviews that you're about to see, we've attempted to make them as close as possible to the exam environment that you will have. There are a couple of small differences:

- In the assessment you are provided with writing materials by the examining body.
- You are not allowed to have a phone in the interview with you because there are clocks in the room. There is a phone on the table in these interviews. That's because I was using it to keep an eye on time. You will not be allowed to have that in the interview itself.

Beyond that, it was as you would expect in the actual assessment. You receive the memo ten minutes before the interview begins and then you have a period of 25 minutes to interview the client. I tried to keep to that; how well I succeed at that, you'll see during the interviews, and I will be doing a reflection on both interviews to summarise my perspective on them and linking what I did to the assessment criteria.

It's important to bear in mind that these are not being held out as perfect interviews. No such thing exists as a perfect interview but it is an interview that hopefully is one that you will see demonstrating some of the techniques, the skills and the goals that I talk about with Amanda in the book. And I will talk in the reflections a little bit about why I believe these would achieve a pass mark in an assessment.

So enjoy the videos. I hope that you enjoy the book and I hope that you all gain from both the book and the videos when it comes to your assessments. Thank you for watching.

## PREPARATION

Hello. This is the introduction to the property interview and, as with the wills interview, I am in the position of having received a memo ten minutes before conducting an interview with a client. Here the client is Joe Smith and the memo is very short, literally four lines, effectively, of substance. So I can't get a huge amount from this.

But let's look at what I can get:

> I've received a telephone call from Joe Smith who needs to speak to us about a property matter.

Well, this adds nothing! I know that this is about a property matter.

> He or she wants to sell the property in the future.

OK, so it's a potential conveyancing matter, but it's unlikely that that's going to be what I'm instructed about specifically today, so I need to bear in the back of my mind that, whatever the client is asking about, the commercial need is to sell. It may be that the property is in negative equity. It may be that there is an urgency to sell; it may be that it's a neighbourhood dispute that means they desperately want to sell. It's potentially not going to be the core of the interview but it is going to be a background consideration.

> and is unsure about some things to do with ownership and boundaries.

Immediately, I'm thinking:

- Is the property registered? Is it unregistered?
- Are they the sole owner or are they joint owners?
- Is there a mortgage?
- Is it anything to do with the title deeds that I'm concerned about?
- Boundaries:
  - Who owns the boundaries?
  - What's the issue?
  - Is the Party Wall [etc.] Act [1996] going to be relevant?
  - Am I going to have to look at joint issues between the parties?

So I have some narrowing down of the issues, but it's not a lot. And in order to get more detail I'm going to have to ask a lot of questions. I'm going to have to let them tell the story to me far more than I do with the wills interview, because with the wills interview the subject matter is very clear. Here, it is not, so I will need to probe more and ask more questions and, crucially, listen to the answers.

## THE INTERVIEW

**Candidate:** Hello? Is it Joe Smith?

**Client:** Yes, that's right.

**Candidate:** Hello, my name's Matthew Parry. I'm a solicitor, a trainee solicitor at the firm here today, and I'm going to be speaking to you about the matter that you've come in to see us about. I understand it's a property matter.

**Client:** Yes. That's right.

**Candidate:** OK, well, hopefully we'll be able to help you through it. I imagine that, if – is it your property that we're talking about, the property you own at the moment?

**Client:** Yes, well, mine and my dad's.

**Candidate:** OK. I imagine it's probably causing you a certain amount of stress.

**Client:** Yes, definitely.

**Candidate:** Property always tends to, so hopefully we'll be able to work our way through that situation and have you at the end of this meeting feeling a little more comfortable, at least, about what your options are.

But thank you for making the time to come and see us today. This is very much your space. It's your interview. So, if you have any questions at any point, don't hesitate to ask. OK?

Just a quick word to lay out the way that this interview is going to go. Have you been to see a solicitor before?

**Client:** Not for a long time.

**Candidate:** OK. Every firm deals with things slightly differently, so I'm just going to quickly explain how the interview is going to go. We've got about 25 minutes for the interview, and at the start I'm going to be saying some really important points that are fairly standard but they are still important because they'll help you to understand how our relationship can work.

And then I'll be asking you to set out the situation, in your own words and in as much detail as you can, so that I can fully understand where you're coming from. Then I'll be asking you some questions. Again, some will be quite detailed; some will be quite personal. When necessary, I'll explain why I'm asking the question but, if you're ever in doubt, please don't hesitate to ask. OK?

And then the really important point, I suspect: I'll give you some legal advice, but also, importantly, I'll try and give you some practical advice, because the practical advice is how you can deal with this situation, either with our help, someone else's help, or possibly by yourself.

**Client:** OK.

**Candidate:** The goal here is that when you leave this interview you feel confident that you have a way forward. I may give you several choices. At the end of the day, the decision is yours. I can advise, I will advise, but at the end of the day it's important to understand that the decision is yours. OK?

**Client:** OK.

**Candidate:** Really important is that everything I say to you is confidential. What that means is, anything you say to me I cannot divulge to anyone outside this firm. There are some exceptions to that – don't worry about them. If it looks like we're reaching a situation where one of those might arise, I will stop, we can talk about it and I'll explain the difficulty.

**Client:** OK.

**Candidate:** But, for now, don't worry about that, all right? In terms of questions, if you don't understand the question, don't hesitate to say. But, again, the really important point is to make sure that you feel comfortable throughout this whole process. Do you have any questions at this particular point?

**Client:** No, I don't think so.

**Candidate:** OK. I'd like to get to know you a little bit better, if possible, so I would really like to find out a bit about you. Where do you live?

**Client:** I live at 17 George Close in Swansea.

**Candidate:** What's the postcode?

**Client:** SA1 1PP.

**Candidate:** OK. And is that the property that's at the heart of this matter?

**Client:** Yes. That's right.

**Candidate:** OK. So we'll be talking a lot about 17 George Close.

**Client:** Yes.

**Candidate:** And what's your full name? Is it Joe Smith?

**Client:** Joe Smith. Yes.

**Candidate:** And how would you like me to address you?

**Client:** Joe is completely fine.

**Candidate:** Please feel free to call me Matthew. In terms of contact details, is writing to you at 17 George Close the best bet?

**Client:** Probably. Actually, telephone is better.

**Candidate:** What's the telephone number?

**Client:** Oh, yes. 07647 512412.

**Candidate:** That's a mobile number. Do you have a landline number, just in case there's an issue with reception or anything?

**Client:** Mobile is the only way, but if you want my email I can give you that as a back-up.

**Candidate:** OK, that's fine.

**Client:** It's Joe.Smith@hotmail.com.

**Candidate:** OK. Thank you very much, that's really helpful. OK, so that covers the issues that I wanted to talk about at the start. There are a few more client care matters that will be put in a letter at the end. And, again, at that point, once you've read it, please don't hesitate to raise any questions you have with me, OK?

**Client:** OK.

**Candidate:** Now, I understand that you want to speak to us about a property matter involving 17 George Close. And I think we were told that you want to sell the property in the future and you're unsure with some things about ownership and boundaries.

**Client:** Yes.

**Candidate:** Can you help me to understand a little more about that? I will be making notes as you speak. The more you can help me, the more I can help you.

**Client:** Yes, sure. Basically, I own this property with my dad, but he unfortunately passed away about a year and a half ago. I'm hoping to sell it sometime soon, because I want to move to London for work, but now my stepsister, Amelia – she basically got everything in my dad's estate when he died – now she's basically coming after me, saying that she's entitled to half the property, that I need to pay her all this money if I sell it, when I sell it. So I'm really concerned about that, from the sale perspective financially.

And then there are also issues with the fences on the property. I'm just worried about the maintenance, especially on the right-hand side, when you're looking at it, the neighbours on the right; I don't think they've been maintaining it very well. The left is all right, but I'm just not sure about it. I just want to make sure I've covered my bases, effectively.

I'd say those are the main points there.

**Candidate:** OK. So effectively the three issues raised are: [1] your stepsister, I think you said. Amelia?

**Client:** Yes, that's right.

**Candidate:** ... who is demanding a contribution from the property itself if and when it's sold; [2] some issues with the right fence; and [3] some issues with the left fence.

**Client:** Yes.

**Candidate:** OK. In terms of what you said, I'm just going to ask a few questions. I think you've given a really good, helpful, broad perspective. I'm going to ask some detailed questions just to get some more – to dive down into it a little more.

You mentioned the property. Do you know if it's registered or not, your property?

**Client:** I don't know. I know we have the title deed and stuff; I'm not sure about the register. My dad mostly dealt with that stuff.

**Candidate:** No, I understand. That's something we can check with the Land Registry. Do you happen to know how the property was held when you bought it? Did your solicitors tell you how it was held?

**Client:** We purchased it jointly, so I believe it's joint tenants in equity there. But I kind of talked with my dad about changing some of the things but I haven't really got around to doing anything about it. So it's still in both of our names now.

**Candidate:** What did those conversations entail? What sort of thing was being said?

**Client:** Basically, he wanted to put my rights in the property so that he would have just 10% of the property and then I would have the rest of it, about 90% of the property. But then his cancer got a lot worse. And we just never really went further into those conversations.

**Candidate:** And I think you said he passed away about a year and a half ago.

**Client:** Yes. That's right.

**Candidate:** I'm sorry again for your loss there.

**Client:** Thank you.

**Candidate:** OK. You said they didn't go any further. There were discussions about it. Was anything put in writing?

**Client:** I don't think so. No.

**Candidate:** OK. Do you know if you spoke to a solicitor about it, or did your father?

**Client:** I don't know if he did. I definitely didn't, though.

**Candidate:** OK. So the impression I'm getting – and please correct me if I'm wrong – is that this was very much at the early stages.

**Client:** Yes, definitely.

**Candidate:** OK. That's helpful, thank you. How much is the property worth?

**Client:** So I would say about £300,000. And then there's also a mortgage of about £250,000.

**Candidate:** OK. How did you come by that valuation, £300,000?

**Client:** We had an evaluator come by.

**Candidate:** OK. If you're going to sell it, that makes sense.

**Client:**      Yes.

**Candidate:**   Normally I leave the legal advice to the second part of the interview after I've gathered all the information. I'm going to do something slightly different because it sounds like this is something that's really concerning you. Is that fair to say?

**Client:**      Yes.

**Candidate:**   And I can understand why. Because if she – how much is she saying that she's entitled to, half?

**Client:**      Half of it. So she wants £150,000.

**Candidate:**   Right. I'm going to deal with that now because of that is something that is concerning you. That is something that, from what you've told me, you don't have to worry about.

**Client:**      OK.

**Candidate:**   And I'm going to say that categorically. There's two reasons for this. The first is, even if she were entitled to half, on the basis that your father had half the property, it would be half of the net amount after the mortgage is paid off. So, even if she were correct on that, the mortgage would be paid off first and she'd be entitled to half of what's left.

**Client:**      OK.

**Candidate:**   That being said, that's only if she's correct that she's entitled to half. From what you've said, you held the property jointly as joint tenants.

**Client:**      Yes.

**Candidate:**   Again, if that is the case, and we will check this with the Land Registry, that means that, once your father sadly passed away, you would own 100% of the house. What he says in his will is irrelevant, which means that Amelia is entitled to nothing.

**Client:**      OK.

**Candidate:**   That's the starting point as I see it; that's where I'm coming from. There is one final point to consider here, and that is that you had conversations about what's called 'severing' the joint tenancy, so that you identified who owns how much.

                 Nothing came of it. If Amelia were able to make an argument to say, 'Actually, I am entitled to that share', she would then only be entitled to the 10%.

**Client:**      OK.

**Candidate:**   Which means it's now down to 10% of effectively 50,000. So it's £5,000. So the sum of £150,000, you don't need to worry about. Does that put your mind at ease a little?

**Client:**      Yes, definitely.

**Candidate:** And I know I said when I was setting out the structure that I would deal with the advice later. I wanted to deal with that now because it's clearly a big point. So I will just go over that again later. But let's move on to the fence issue. You said the right fence as you look at the property?

**Client:** Yes.

**Candidate:** You mentioned it's not in great repair. Can you tell me a bit about that?

**Client:** Yes. Basically the neighbours on the right, they just haven't been maintaining it. The main issue with that is that their dog keeps escaping onto the property. So I'm just concerned about what that means for me.

**Candidate:** What has the impact been of the dog coming onto your property?

**Client:** I mean, it's not a huge impact because it's a smaller dog, but it'll come on and, you know, do its business on the lawn effectively before the neighbours are able to chase it back to their property.

**Candidate:** Has the dog done any damage to your property? Apart from doing his business, has the dog done any damage to your property?

**Client:** No. Aside from, you know, the little hole in the fence. Otherwise, nothing, no.

**Candidate:** Again, this may be a question you can't answer but, based on your memory of when you bought the property, did your solicitor at the time tell you who is responsible for maintaining those fences?

**Client:** No, I don't recall.

**Candidate:** No, that's absolutely—that's something we can look into. OK. Have you spoken to your neighbours about this?

**Client:** Yes. Because I was - for a long time, I was sure that they owned it, that they owned the fence, but they've pushed back on that, that they don't actually own it, so we're not quite sure. And they're taking a laissez-faire approach with the dog. So I have not really had any luck with them.

**Candidate:** OK. And just one - is there one hole in the fence? Are there multiple holes?

**Client:** It's just the one, yes; the one hole where the dog sneaks in. The rest of the fence is just not in the best condition.

**Candidate:** OK. If the hole were to be fixed by whoever, about how much would it cost, do you think? I mean, I'm not asking for a DIY expert's quote here!

**Client:** I don't know; maybe £100?

**Candidate:** OK. And obviously the rest of the fence, if that would be repaired, would be slightly more expensive?

**Client:** Yes, definitely.

**Candidate:** OK. You mentioned the left fence as you look at the property. What's the situation there?

**Client:** I'm pretty sure that I maintain it well. I'm just worried that buyers aren't going to like what I've done with it, especially if it's in a different condition to the right side, if it's lopsided or something like that.

**Candidate:** It sounds like your main concern here is about selling the property – is that right?

**Client:** Yes.

**Candidate:** You mentioned that when you explained why you were here. You said that a few times. What is the situation with selling the property?

**Client:** I want to sell because I do want to go to London eventually. I would like the money from the property. Of course, currently I'm trying to save a bunch of money so that I can go to London, but hoping to sell it maybe in the next year or so.

**Candidate:** Right. So your plan is to sell. What are your concerns with selling? Because a lot of these issues seem to be linked to that.

**Client:** Yes: how much the fence is going to affect how much I can sell the property for, and what to do with [the fences]. And then there's one other thing: there's a birdbath in the back garden that's cemented into the ground, but it was carved by my dad, so I'm hoping to take that with me, and wondering if I'm able to do that when I sell the property.

**Candidate:** OK. I can fully understand it. So what's the approximate value of that, would you say?

**Client:** I'm not sure. I don't know what he carved it with but it looks expensive at least.

**Candidate:** And if it's carved by your dad, I'm guessing it potentially has more value to you than it might to other people.

**Client:** Definitely. I wouldn't want to sell it.

**Candidate:** OK. No, I can fully appreciate that. You said it's concreted into the ground. Any idea how deep it is? Is it fairly clearly fixed there?

**Client:** Yes, I would say so. It's quite a large birdbath there, yes.

**Candidate:** How easy would it be to excavate it, do you think? And again I understand you're not a—

**Client:** Probably if I got some buddies around, we could probably do it. I'm not sure it would take a big machine or anything to take it out, but it would definitely be a bit of a process to take it out.

**Candidate:** OK, I fully understand. It sounds very much as though you're looking to get everything shipshape, into order, so that you can sell it with as few issues as possible.

**Client:** That's right.

**Candidate:** Is it fair to say that that's your main concern here?

**Client:**    Yes.

**Candidate:**  OK. But all of these issues obviously are important within their own rights as well.

**Client:**    Yes.

**Candidate:**  OK. Are there any other issues that you want to ask about, or any other concerns that you have?

**Client:**    It's not really an issue but, since I'm saving up to go to London, I'm wondering if in the lead-up to me selling, am I able to stop paying the mortgage before I sell?

**Candidate:**  So the mortgage is another question as well. Who's the mortgage with?

**Client:**    With me.

**Candidate:**  I'm sorry – which of the banks? Santander, or ... ?

**Client:**    I think it's Santander.

**Candidate:**  Santander. OK. No problem. So is there anything else that you think might be useful to help me understand the situation?

**Client:**    I don't think so. I think that's all the information I can [provide]. If something else comes up, I'll let you know.

**Candidate:**  And just a few more details, just so I've got them. The neighbours on your right as you look at the property, the ones with the dog. What sort of dog is it, by the way?

**Client:**    Yorkshire terrier.

**Candidate:**  Yorkshire terrier. So quite small, can slip through gaps.

**Client:**    That's right.

**Candidate:**  I won't ask if you've got a photo. So you're 17; are they 19? Are they 15 George Close?

**Client:**    They'd be 19.

**Candidate:**  They're 19. What are the names of the people who own the property?

**Client:**    It's Roseanne and Josephine who own it.

**Candidate:**  Roseanne and Josephine. Surname?

**Client:**    I want to say Daryl but I'm not sure.

**Candidate:**  We can look that up. And the other side would then be 13?

**Client:**    Yes, that's right.

**Candidate:**  And the names of the people who own that property?

**Client:**        That's Jim, and his wife is, I think it's Sarah.

**Candidate:** No problem. Is that S-A-R-A or S-A-R-A-H?

**Client:**        Sarah with an 'h'.

**Candidate:** OK. We can look up their details easily enough, but obviously having the contact details helps. So, just to summarise what you've told us, and please do feel free to correct me if I've missed anything here: you purchased 17 George Close about how long ago?

**Client:**        Maybe five years ago.

**Candidate:** About five years ago. And how much did you pay for it, approximately? It's now worth £300,000, you said.

**Client:**        Yes, I think; gosh, I don't really remember. Maybe around £200,000, we paid for it.

**Candidate:** OK. It's gone up considerably.

**Client:**        Yes.

**Candidate:** So you purchased it for £200,000 with your father, who sadly is no longer with us. He passed away about a year and a half ago. And, crucially, you want to sell the property. You've got a number of issues that you want to resolve. The first is your stepsister, Amelia, who believes she's entitled to half the value. The second is the neighbours to your right – that's 19 George Close – because their dog escapes into your garden. It's annoying to you and you're concerned it would put off buyers. The neighbours on the left, number 13, Jim and Sarah. And that's more about not [being] sure what you are allowed to do to the fence and whether or not anyone would be happy. The fourth issue is whether you can stop paying the mortgage on the basis that you want to sell the property. And the fifth issue is the birdbath in the back garden that is concreted in.

**Client:**        Yes.

**Candidate:** And those are the five issues that you've come for advice on?

**Client:**        Yes, definitely.

**Candidate:** OK. Have I missed anything crucial from that summary?

**Client:**        I don't think so, no.

**Candidate:** OK. And your primary concern is making sure that this is in the best possible position to be sold?

**Client:**        That's right.

**Candidate:** OK. Covering the issues – I'm going to go through them one by one – we've dealt with Amelia and that issue. Just to remind you, the starting point seems to be joint tenancy. Therefore, the property went into your sole ownership when your father sadly passed away. But because there were discussions to sever the tenancy anyway, even if she were entitled to anything, it would be far, far less. But at the moment it doesn't look like anything reached a sufficient level. That's something we can check by looking at the title deeds, and that will cost the grand sum of £3 to get them off Land Registry if it's registered! If it's not registered, we'll have to go and get some documents, which either you'll have or the bank will have copies of.

**Client:** OK.

**Candidate:** And, again, we can deal with that.

**Client:** And that wouldn't impact anything with Amelia, if it's registered or not?

**Candidate:** No, that doesn't impact anything at all. The crucial question is: is it joint tenancy or not? If it's joint tenancy, you own all the property, subject to the mortgage company.

**Client:** OK.

**Candidate:** In terms of the mortgage company, if we segue to there: you are contractually obliged to make the mortgage payments up to the point that the property is sold.

**Client:** OK.

**Candidate:** If you stop paying, you will effectively be in breach of contract with them and they will be able to potentially repossess the property from you. So my advice would be: keep paying the mortgage.

**Client:** And that until it's sold, not listed?

**Candidate:** Not until it's listed; until it's actually sold. And, that way, no issues with Santander.

**Client:** Got it.

**Candidate:** I appreciate I'm not giving you a huge range of options at the moment! That's simply because these are quite straightforward issues in that respect. Now, when it comes to the fence – let's talk about the birdbath first, then we'll come back to the fence. The birdbath: at the moment, you can do whatever you want with the birdbath. It's yours. So, if you want to remove it, you can remove it. It sounds as though it's what is called a fixture. Now, that means if you do sell the property, it would potentially be sold with the property. So, when you take the things that you want to take with you when you leave, this would have to stay. But, until you sell the property, it's yours. You can do what you want with it. So my advice would be potentially, look to remove it before you start [showing] people around. That means you can then fill in the hole and make it look nice and pretty for them again. And there's no expectation about that. Obviously it's up to you what you want to do about that: how easy it is to move, how difficult it is to move, how expensive it would be to remove, whether you're going to have somewhere in London, potentially, that you're going to be able to put it. But that's very much an aesthetic decision for you rather than a legal one. Legally, at the moment it's yours to do with as you want. If it came to a sale, it would probably be a fixture. So, if you still had it there when you were [selling], make sure you tell the buyer that you're taking it with you, so that it can be put in the contract, right?

**Client:**    Right.

**Candidate:**    The fence: both fences effectively will be similar. Who has responsibility for that will be set out in the documents when you bought the property.

**Client:**    Right.

**Candidate:**    There are three options: it could be your own responsibility; it could be your neighbours', or it could be what's called a party wall, which means you both have joint responsibility.

**Client:**    OK.

**Candidate:**    So if it's your responsibility, it's your responsibility. In which case you would be responsible for maintaining both fences, including keeping it so a dog doesn't come through. If it's theirs, it's their legal responsibility, and you do have options. You can complain to them, which it sounds like you've tried to do but without any [success]. You could, if you wanted to, seek legal proceedings against them, which would mean you could issue a claim and say: 'You are required to maintain this fence; you have not done that. I require you to do it or to pay for compensation for the losses.'

**Client:**    Right.

**Candidate:**    Going down the court route is very expensive; that's the drawback. The advantage is, you might get this issue settled once and for all. The downside is it can take time; it can take money.

**Client:**    But I could just tell them I've been to a solicitor?

**Candidate:**    Yes, or you can tell them that. You can go to them and say, 'Look, I've been to the solicitor. They told me this.' The way we can find out for sure how these fences are held is by looking at the original title documentation. So we can do that quite quickly and tell you what the situation is.

**Client:**    Perfect.

**Candidate:**    You can do all that: you can speak to them; you can try to negotiate with them. This is where you have options. Which option you choose is whichever one [works] best for you. The other option that I should bring to your attention – simply because you've said that selling it is your priority – regardless of whose ownership it is, you may want to consider simply repairing it yourself.

**Client:**    Right.

**Candidate:**    To ensure that the matter is dealt with, particularly as I think you said it would cost about £100.

**Client:**    Probably, yes.

**Candidate:**    That would also of course get rid of the dog situation immediately. But, as I say, you do potentially have some rights against your neighbours there.

In terms of the left, it doesn't sound like there are any particular issues there apart from, if it is owned by them, they're entitled to complain if they don't like what you've done with it. Have there been any complaints?

**Client:**       No. I think just because the right side has been such an issue, I'm just worried about the left as well.

**Candidate:**   And, again, it's useful then to make sure we know who does have the legal responsibility. And then that's something that will be useful when you come to sell, because you can then tell the buyer who actually does have the right.

But, as I say, this is where you do have options, particularly in the right-hand fence. You can complain, you can potentially write to them, you can have us write to them on your behalf. Again, these all have advantages. The main disadvantage is cost: if you use our services, we'll have to charge you. Likewise, if you go to court it can be timely and expensive. So a lot will depend on what the crucial thing for you is, which sounds like just getting rid of the issue so that it's ready to sell. The sooner the issue is dealt with, obviously the sooner you can start marketing it.

**Client:**       Right.

**Candidate:**   I appreciate I have given a lot of information here. Are you clear with the advice that I've given?

**Client:**       I think so, yes. I think it all makes sense.

**Candidate:**   Just to summarise, because we will put this in writing for you: Amelia – we'll check the title documents if you instruct us to, but it sounds like the property is yours. You don't have to worry about her. If she wants to pursue you for the different amount of money, that's something we can deal with.

**Client:**       OK.

**Candidate:**   In terms of the mortgage, you are legally obligated to keep paying the mortgage. If you don't, obviously they can't force you to but if you don't, they can potentially pursue you for damages and potentially look to repossess the property. So the advice there would be very much: pay the mortgage.

The birdbath, we've explained: it's yours at the moment, but if the property were to be sold with it still there it could be a fixture and then be part of the sale. So, again, clarity is important with any purchaser.

The fences: it will depend on who has the legal ownership. That's something we can look at.

**Client:**       OK.

**Candidate:**   Are you clear with everything we've set out?

**Client:**       Yes, I think so.

**Candidate:**   Do you feel more comfortable now than when you came in, with your options?

**Client:**       Definitely. Especially about Amelia. It's good to know.

**Candidate:**   That's good. I would not normally be so definitive, but from what you've said, it sounds very clear because the property was held as joint tenants.

**Client:**      OK.

**Candidate:** Going forward, if you can provide us with any documents that you have, that would be useful just so we can look into it to see exactly what the legal position is. We will write to you with a client care letter, which will set out everything that we discussed. It will set out contact details, my contact details, contact details of colleagues in case I'm not available, the fees that we'll charge if you wish to instruct us going forward, and also a complaints procedure in case you have any concerns that you wish to raise.

**Client:**      OK.

**Candidate:** OK? And please do not hesitate to get in touch if you'd like to talk about this in any sense. If you did want to use us going forward, the logical next step would be to get access to the title documentation if you don't have a copy, so that we can see exactly what the legal situation is. I suspect it will confirm a lot of what we've said, however. Is that clear?

**Client:**      Yes, I think so.

**Candidate:** Do you have any other questions?

**Client:**      No, I think that's everything.

**Candidate:** Well, thank you very much for coming in. If you do remember anything at the last minute, don't hesitate to drop us an email. We will be charging at the hourly rate that we'll talk about in the letter going forward. But obviously if you need to clarify anything about what we've said, please do get in touch – and good luck with the sale. I hope I do see you in the future.

**Client:**      Thanks so much.

**Candidate:** Thank you very much and don't hesitate to get in touch.

## REFLECTION

This is the reflection on the property interview that I've just conducted with Joe Smith, with Hayley playing the role of Joe again. And again, as with the wills interview, I'm going to reflect on it in two parts, first of all talking about my feelings about the interview, and the second talking about the assessment criteria. Again, just a reminder: this is not held out as a perfect interview but it is held out as the sort of interview that would hopefully pass on the assessment criteria. And I'll talk about that in a moment.

So how did the interview go from my perspective? Well, the first thing to say – the elephant in the room – is those of you keeping an eye on the time would have seen that it was over 25 minutes. I didn't have access to a clock but you will. So at 25 minutes you will be cut off by the assessor.

So don't make the mistake that I did:

• Keep an eye on the time.
• Know when you're coming up to the end of your time; realistically you want to be stopping talking by about 24 minutes so that you can conclude, you can wrap up the interview gently, without rushing.

- What you don't want to do is to be cut off at 25 minutes, because it will make you feel bad even if you still pass the assessment. Just because you get cut off does not mean you're going to fail, but you will be thinking 'have I missed some points?'

So how could I have saved the 2.5 minutes that I ran over? Well, some of my questioning ran on a little. I repeated a few points. I went into perhaps unnecessary detail. None of these things are disastrous but they are things that will add time to your interview. So try to be as clear, as succinct, as precise as you can be.

What went well? I think I adapted my approach effectively. As you will know from the book, one of the suggestions in terms of structure and the structure that I said to the client was to ask questions, gather the information and then give legal advice. Here, I broke that. On a particular issue, I gave advice before I gathered all the information. I took that decision because it was clear that the client was concerned about it, and I had the information I needed to give an informed decision. So I adapted. And one of the really important things about a skill such as this is knowing when to break your own rules. It's about the client. In this situation, I felt it was justified and I would absolutely do that again. It was one of the reasons that it ran over, because I then repeated that advice later. That was still important to underpin the advice, because it remained an important issue. But, again, it's an area that I could have saved some time.

Generally speaking, I thought the interview went well. I allowed the client the chance to express. I could perhaps have cut down the opening slightly but I allowed the client the chance to set out the story and then to hear what she said and ask appropriate questions. And the legal advice? While somewhat prescriptive at times, where I had the chance to give options I took that, and I gave the client the options. What I could have done was express more clearly that the decision as to what to do was their choice, and to ask what their feeling was at the moment. But, overall, I thought it was a successful interview, even though it ran long.

Looking at the assessment criteria:

1. Listen to the client and use questioning effectively to enable the client to tell the solicitor what is important to them.
   Yes: I used open and closed questions to get the information that I needed. The client did not feel rushed.
2. Communicate and explain in a way that is suitable for the client to understand.
   Again, I used language that was clear. I made it clear what I needed them to do and what I would do.
3. Conduct themselves in a professional manner and treat the client with courtesy, respect and politeness including respecting diversity where relevant.
   Professionalism, I don't think, was an issue.
4. Demonstrate client-focus in the approach to the client and the issues.
   The focus was very much on: what is *your* main concern? How can we resolve that?
5. Establish and maintain an effective relationship with the client so as to build trust and confidence.
   That was something that was tended to throughout.

So, although it ran long, the assessment criteria I believe was met here. But in your situation do please keep a clear eye on the time because someone will intervene and cut you off at 25 minutes and that, even if it doesn't affect your mark, will make you more nervous and concerned ahead of the remainder of your assessments.

But, in this situation, I did feel that I met the assessment criteria and that I had sufficient information to be able to write an attendance note on it immediately afterwards.

# ■ SAMPLE ATTENDANCE NOTE/LEGAL ANALYSIS

## Meeting with Joe Smith re forthcoming property sale

**Date:**     DD/MM/YY
**Time:**     10.00–10.25
**Client:**   Joe Smith
**Matter:**   Property sale

Client attended to ask for advice about a number of concerns that she has in respect of the property and that she wants to address before selling. Client is concerned about the amount of money that she will gain from the property in the event of a sale and wants clarification.

The property was purchased jointly with her father who has recently died. The property remains in joint names; client and deceased were joint tenants. Current value is approx. £300,000 with a mortgage of approx. £250,000 so there is around £50,000 equity.

Client's queries:

1.  Who is entitled to the equity?
2.  Can a stone birdbath be removed or is it part of the property?
3.  Issues with fences.
4.  Mortgage payment.

### Advice

1.  Equity

The client's stepsister, who inherited from their father's estate, has claimed half the value of the property (£150,000). Client is very concerned. However, client is entitled to the property as they held it as joint tenants and so the property falls outside the estate.

Client and deceased had discussed severing the joint tenancy, with a 90/10 split in favour of client. This was never finalised. The starting point is that the joint tenancy remains.

There could be an argument that there was severance by mutual agreement, and I advised that the law was mixed on whether the actions to date had been enough. More information would be needed.

However, the severance intention was to leave only 10% to her father, and so at most the stepsister's claim would be 10% of the approximately £50,000 equity. I advised that the stepsister's claim for £150,000 was not a good claim. Client was relieved.

2.  Stone birdbath

A stone birdbath is cemented into the back garden (installed by client's father). It holds sentimental value and client asked whether she could take it with her when she moved.

Explained that she could do whatever she chooses – subject to being able to move the birdbath (which was outside my competence). I explained that if it was still there when the house was sold it may be seen as a fixture and so part of the sale. Discussions with purchaser would then be needed.

3.  Fences

Fences to right: client thinks neighbours own it. Their dogs escape to client's garden. Fences to left: client thinks she owns it. Neighbours may not be happy with work.

Advised that the fence ownership would be set out in the plan on the title deeds; advised looking at that for clarity (easy and cheap process to obtain the plans). In follow-up letter I should clarify that if she wants the firm to review the plans, this would involve a cost.

In the meantime, advised client to speak to the neighbours on the left to see if they have any objections to her fence plans.

On the right, advised that neighbours may be liable for damages as it is their dog and, potentially, their responsibility to mend the fence. However, to deal with the situation now, advised putting a temporary block on the fence and speaking to the neighbours about how to address the long-term situation.

4.  Can the client stop paying the mortgage as she knows she wants to sell?

Advised that the mortgage obligations continue until such point as it is paid off. Stopping payments could lead to action from the lender. Strongly advised against.

### Next steps for client and for firm
1.  Send a client care letter to client with record of advice.
2.  Ask for instructions (and funds) to acquire title docs and plans.
3.  Wait on instructions in respect of neighbours.

## COMMENTARY

On balance, the candidate has met the threshold standard for the attendance note/legal analysis component of the SQE2 client interview assessment:

*   **AC 1** Record all relevant information: The candidate has included key facts set out in the assessment documents and elicited in the client interview, in particular the range of concerns that the client has, the details of these concerns and the advice given.
*   **AC 2** Identify appropriate next steps: The candidate has identified that they would write to Joe setting out the advice and next steps, and had understood the limits of what they can do.
*   **AC 3** Provide client-focused advice: The candidate has demonstrated an understanding of the client's concerns from the client's perspective, for example that Joe is very concerned about the demand for £150,000, and that there are sentimental reasons behind the birdbath. The candidate has also understood the overall goal, which is to sell the property.
*   **AC 4** Apply the law correctly: The candidate has identified the relevant fundamental legal principles and applied them correctly to the facts of the client's case. The client has identified the crucial tests for fixtures and fittings, severance of a joint tenancy, mortgage obligations and ownership.
*   **AC 5** Apply the law comprehensively: The candidate's advice is sufficiently detailed in the context of the factual issues. For example, the candidate has explained the limitations of any claim by the stepsister and the fact that even if the joint tenancy has been severed the claim will be lower. There was awareness of the practical application of fixture and fitting rules, and how the boundary dispute will arise.

# ■ SUMMARY AND REFLECTION

One of the crucial points to note from the interview is the importance of clarifying the relevant issues as quickly as possible. Unlike the wills and probate interview, where it is possible to gauge what the areas might be from the will that you are provided with, there is potentially far less information available ahead of the property interview. Therefore, by identifying the client's questions at an early stage of the interview, you will give yourself the best opportunity to cover all matters and not miss anything.

Finally, try to make sure that your questions focus not just on what the client is seeking but also the impact that this will have on them. For example, in this interview, the client wanted raw information about the estate but the impact of the candidate's answers had the potential to be significant. The client was scared about the demand for £150,000 and had an emotional attachment to the statue. There will be a temptation to emphasise your empathy and emotional tools in the wills and probate interview but it is just as important here. Remember the assessment criteria for client interviewing: in order to achieve **AC 3**, **AC 4** and **AC 5**, you will need to demonstrate your focus on the client's perspective and sensitivity towards their concerns, so that you can establish and maintain an effective, professional relationship with the client.

# Final words

We hope that the guidance and examples contained in this book have helped to put into context how to use your practice skills to ensure you reach the SQE2 grading criteria. Remember, above all, this is an assessment and the examiner needs to see evidence that you have met the assessment criteria in order for you to pass the threshold. Always keep this in the back of your mind when taking your SQE2 assessments.

Whilst this book is designed to aid your learning and provide helpful tips on how to pass your SQE2 assessments, it is no substitute for practice. All skills are improved with repetition and refining your technique, and legal skills are no exception to this rule. Take any opportunity you can to practise your interviewing and writing skills. Reflect carefully on your performance after each exercise:

- What could you have done better?
- Did you meet all of the grading criteria applicable to that particular skill?
- Do you need to fill any gaps in your legal knowledge?

Constant practice and self-reflection are the keys to success.

Finally, the team at *Revise SQE* wish you the best of luck in your SQE2 assessments!

# Appendix

## PERFORMANCE INDICATORS FOR SQE2 CLIENT INTERVIEWING ASSESSMENT CRITERIA

| Skills | Indicators demonstrating competence | Indicators that do not demonstrate competence |
|---|---|---|
| Listen to the client and use questioning effectively to enable the client to tell the solicitor what is important to them. | • The candidate demonstrates active listening skills and engagement with the client, for example by<br>  ○ listening attentively (use of facial expressions/body language/tone of voice/may evidence this)<br>  ○ avoiding interrupting the client<br>  ○ listening without judgement<br>  ○ avoiding making assumptions<br>• The candidate asks appropriate questions (e.g. questions designed to elicit relevant information from the client)<br>• The candidate uses a combination of open and closed questions. An open question is a question which invites the client to share more detailed information e.g. it could be a question beginning with the words 'tell me about the property you would like to buy . . .' Closed questions could be questions where the response would be 'yes' or 'no' e.g. 'Do you own your own property') | • The candidate appears disinterested (e.g. facial expressions/body language/tone of voice indicate a lack of engagement with the client)<br>• The candidate appears distracted/reluctant to address the client's concerns (e.g. tied to their own agenda/over reliant on their notes/repeating information the client has already provided/interrupting the client)<br>• The candidate does not ask appropriate or relevant questions<br>• The candidate uses only closed questions or does not use sufficient/appropriate open questions, which prevents the client from explaining what is important to them |

| Skills | Indicators demonstrating competence | Indicators that do not demonstrate competence |
|---|---|---|
| Communicate and explain in a way that is suitable for the client to understand. | • The candidate uses language which is easily understood by the client<br>• Where it is necessary to use technical language that a client would not understand, the candidate explains the legal terms clearly and succinctly (e.g. 'restrictive covenant'; 'legal easement'; 'age contingency'; 'nil rate band') | • The candidate's explanations are verbose, legalistic, complicated, rambling or confused and not understood by the client<br>• The candidate uses technical language when necessary but provides little, if any, explanation and/or the explanations provided are vague, even when questioned by the client |
| Conduct themselves in a professional manner and treat the client with courtesy, respect and politeness including respecting diversity where relevant. | • The candidate imparts difficult or unwelcome news clearly and with sensitivity<br>• The candidate treats the client with courtesy and respect<br>• The candidate behaves politely and builds rapport with the client<br>• The candidate's behaviour achieves the right balance of professional distance whilst being interested in the client's problem<br>• The candidate maintains control of the interview (e.g. the candidate is well organised; calm, composed and efficient, and does not appear rushed) | • The candidate's behaviour towards the client is consistently insensitive<br>• The candidate has an overly familiar, casual, or highly informal manner e.g. the candidate is flippant or makes jokes with client<br>• The candidate's behaviour is rude; abrupt; dismissive; disrespectful; judgemental; or patronizing<br>• The candidate is hesitant throughout or lacking in confidence; appears rushed and flustered; is not in control of the interview |
| Demonstrate client-focus in their approach to the client and the issues (i.e. demonstrate an understanding of the problem from the client's point of view and what the client wants to achieve, not just from a legal perspective). | • The candidate demonstrates an understanding of the client's problem from the client's perspective (e.g. the candidate addresses the client's legal problem, any relevant commercial considerations and/or the client's personal circumstances)<br>• The candidate acknowledges and responds to the client's concerns with interest and empathy | • The candidate does not approach or appreciate the client's problem from the client's perspective<br>• The candidate does not respond to the client's concerns with interest and empathy<br>• The candidate provides advice which does not take into account the client's aims or concerns |
| Establish and maintain an effective relationship with the client so as to build trust and confidence. | • The candidate effectively manages the client's expectations/circumstances, e.g. balances the client's objectives against what can be achieved within the timeframe; the client feels confident that the matter is in good hands and will be progressed | • The candidate fails to manage the client's expectations/ circumstances and the client would have little or no confidence that the matter will be progressed; the client would not want to entrust the matter to the solicitor |

# PERFORMANCE INDICATORS FOR SQE2 CLIENT ATTENDANCE NOTE/LEGAL ANALYSIS ASSESSMENT CRITERIA

| Skills | Indicators demonstrating competence | Indicators that do not demonstrate competence |
|---|---|---|
| Record all relevant information | • The candidate identifies and sets out the relevant facts contained in the assessment documents and elicited from the Client Interview, e.g. facts which are important in ensuring the client's needs/objectives are met or relevant to the legal analysis | • The candidate does not identify relevant facts from the assessment documents, or elicited from the Client Interview, which meet the client's objectives or are relevant to their legal analysis<br>• The candidate includes many facts in their answer which have no bearing on their legal advice |
| Identify appropriate next steps | • The candidate sets out the steps to be taken to progress the client's matter, e.g. the solicitor will provide a letter of advice to the client, or request further information from the client | • The candidate does not set out any relevant next steps to progress the client's matter<br>• The candidate sets out next steps which do not progress the client's matter, e.g. recommending lines of enquiry which have no bearing on the client's problem |
| Provide client focused advice (ie advice which demonstrates an understanding of the problem from the client's point of view and what the client wants to achieve, not just from a legal perspective) | • The candidate demonstrates an understanding of the client's concerns from the client's perspective (e.g. the candidate addresses the client's legal problems, any relevant commercial considerations and/or the client's personal circumstances). | • The candidate does not approach or appreciate the client's problem from the client's perspective, e.g. produces a legal analysis which does not take into account the client's concerns. |
| Law | Indicators demonstrating competence | Indicators that do not demonstrate competence |
| Apply the law correctly to the client's situation | • The candidate identifies the relevant fundamental legal principles in accordance with the SQE2 assessment specification and applies them correctly to the facts of the client's case | • The candidate does not identify and correctly apply the relevant legal principles to the facts of the client's case<br>• The candidate does not apply the relevant legal principles in a way that addresses the client's needs and concerns |
| Apply the law comprehensively to the client's situation, identifying any ethical and professional conduct issues and exercising judgement to resolve them honestly and with integrity | • The candidate's attendance note and legal analysis is sufficiently detailed in the context of the client's case and the relevant factual and legal issues<br>• Where relevant, the candidate recognises ethical issues and exercises effective judgement in addressing them in accordance with the SRA Principles and rules of professional conduct | • The candidate's attendance note and legal analysis is not sufficiently detailed in the context of the client's case and the relevant factual and legal issues<br>• The candidate does not recognise ethical issues or exercise effective judgement in addressing them in accordance with the SRA Principles and rules of professional conduct |

# Index